Curtains and blinds

in a weekend

Curtains and blinds

in a weekend

Jacqueline Venning

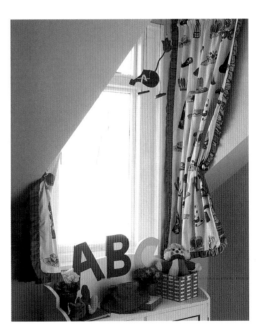

MEREHURST

Acknowledgements

Thanks are due to my family for putting up with all the upheaval that this book has caused; particularly my daughter Sarah, who, as a newly married career woman with (I am ashamed to say) absolutely no sewing skills, checked the viability of each project. Also to my friends who let me use their window settings; Linda White for her delicate and detailed artwork; Dominic Blackmore for his patience with the photography; Nel Lintern for her inspired choice of accessories; and Sara Colledge at Merehurst Fairfax for putting it all together.

First published 1997 by Merehurst Limited,
Ferry House, 51-57 Lacy Road, London, SW15 1PR

ISBN 1-85391-539-4

A catalogue record for this book is available from the British Library.

Editor: Geraldine Christy
Designer: Anthony Cohen
Photographer: Dominic Blackmore
Stylist: Nel Lintern
Artworks: Linda White/Brihton Illustration

Colour separation by Bright Arts, Hong Kong
Printed in Italy by New InterLitho S.p.A.

Contents

Introduction

A new home and only a little spare time. How do you make your house or flat into a home and give it that individual touch? Having the right curtains and blinds is a very good starting point. The window is often the focal point of a room and is always a major decorative and design feature. In your choice of curtains and blinds you can set the style and feel of a room, whether it is in the town or the country, of traditional or modern style and whether it is for work or relaxation.

For those new to soft furnishing and craft work generally, furnishing a home can be a daunting prospect and doing this alongside a demanding job or bringing up young children can be an even more awesome task. Many people these days may find this complicated by having to move house every few years. Ideas and fashions also change regularly and while today's look is simple and clean-cut you may soon desire a new look and be keen to create it as soon as you can.

Do choose a colour scheme to suit the aspect, function and mood of the room. Use warm colours such as yellows and apricots for cold and dark rooms. Pale blues and greens are lovely in light and sunny rooms, and they will also give the room a spacious and relaxed feeling, whereas vibrant colours such as reds suggest activity and business. But whatever you do choose for an individual room, remember to have one neutral shade: a cream, beige or even white carrying from room to room throughout the house. Rooms should not be too perfectly colour co-ordinated though, because they will be bland and uninteresting. Always add an accent colour as a wild gesture: for example, one red cushion in a mainly pale room will give the room instant impact.

I have designed the projects in this book so that they are as easy as possible for you to make, giving you a wide range of ideas but not too much to cope with. There are suggestions on window dressings for a variety of different window shapes and settings, as well as tips on choosing the most suitable fabrics. There are also lists of the equipment and materials that you will need for each project, and finally there are step-by-step instructions on how to make the curtains and blinds.

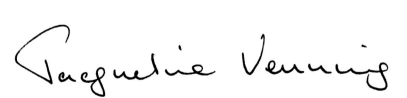

The methods used to make up the window dressings described in this book have deliberately been kept as simple as possible. I have tried to use tracks and fittings that are readily available; you will not have to search for specialist shops. So by preparing well in advance and following the instructions for any one of these projects, even those of you with very little practical experience and a busy lifestyle will be able to change a room, giving it your own individual look, and all in a weekend.

Jacqueline Venning

Unlined curtains with a variety of headings

A pair of simple, unlined curtains are quick to make and are an easy way to make an enormous difference to a room. The fabric you choose will determine the final effect.

Consider the effect you are hoping to achieve when buying your material. Fine fabrics such as voiles and muslins will float and billow, glazed chintzes will be crisp and firm (though sometimes unyielding), and cottons will fold and drape well (the size of the folds depends on the thickness of the fabric).

The designs described for this project have been chosen to suit curtains that require only a minimum amount of fullness and therefore need little fabric. The taped heading can be adapted, however, to have more of a gather, simply by using an extra width of fabric. The curtain can also be made to appear more 'fussy' by allowing extra fabric above the tape, thus giving a frilled effect. This heading is also suitable for an 'overlong' curtain; that is, one in which the hem drags along the floor.

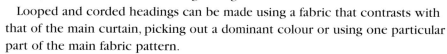

Looped and corded headings can be made using a fabric that contrasts with that of the main curtain, picking out a dominant colour or using one particular part of the main fabric pattern.

The Day One instructions explain how to make the basic curtains. When you have decided which heading you prefer, follow the specific Day Two instructions on how to finish the curtains.

Planning your time

DAY ONE
AM: Fix pole above window

PM: Cut out fabric, machine sew all seams and hems

DAY TWO
AM: Design curtain heading

PM: Sew on tape or make headings, hang curtains

Tools and materials

Curtain fabric

Matching sewing threads

Curtain pole

A strip of card 4 cm (1½ in) wide

A strip of card 7.5 cm (3 in) wide

Sewing kit

Sewing machine

Metre ruler and metal tape measure

Iron and ironing board

Drill and screwdriver etc. for fitting pole

Curtain rings and hooks (for taped heading only)

4–5 m (4½–5½ yd) narrow curtain tape (for taped heading only)

30–40 brass eyelets and fitting tool (for rope heading only)

Button twine (for rope heading only)

Rope or cord, approximately 3 times the length of the pole (for rope heading only)

Preparation

Decide upon the length of the pole and where on the wall it is to be fixed (see below). Measure up for the curtain fabric (see below).

Measuring for curtain pole

The pole should extend the length of the window recess plus an extra 15 cm (6 in) on each side (less on small windows, slightly more on larger ones).

Positioning the pole

The ideal fixing place for a pole from which to hang full length curtains is at a point halfway between the ceiling and the top of the window recess. On smaller windows, however, this is not always possible and in some situations does not look right at all. Ideally, the pole should be fixed as high above the window as the curtains are to hang below it but there must always be at least 10 cm (4 in) between the bottom of the pole and the top of the window recess.

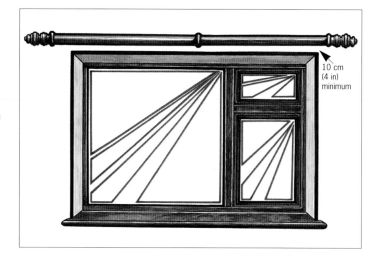

Measuring up for fabric

Length of fabric required

Taped headings: Measure from the bottom of the pole to the floor – this is the drop. To this measurement, add 20 cm (8 in) for hems and turnings. If the curtains are to be 'overlong', add 10–15 cm (4–6 in) more and if there is to be a frilled effect above the curtain tape, add a further 10–20 cm (4–8 in), according to the size of the frilling.

Looped and corded headings: Measure from just below the pole to the floor (or to the proposed finish of the curtain) to obtain the drop measurement. Then add 20 cm (8 in) for hems and turnings.

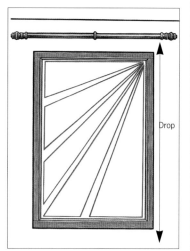

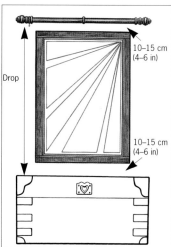

Width of fabric required

A simple, unlined curtain requires a fullness of approximately 1½ times the length of the pole. Therefore, a window which is 150 cm (59 in) wide and which has a 180 cm (71 in) pole fitted, will only require two widths of fabric 137 cm (54 in) wide (see Terms and techniques – Furnishing fabrics). A longer pole will require a third width of fabric.

Quantity of fabric required

This is worked out by multiplying the overall length measurement by the number of widths required. Allowance should also be made for the pattern to match across the widths (see Terms and techniques – Pattern repeats).

Loop and cord-headed curtains will require an extra 50 cm (19¾ in) to make the tabs and borders. This can be of a contrasting fabric or of the main fabric.

Day One
Step 1

Put up the curtain pole (see page 10). Cut the curtain fabric to the required length by measuring the drop and adding an allowance of 20 cm (8 in) for hems and turnings, as well as allowances for any further designs or patterns (see Measuring up for fabric on page 10 and Terms and techniques – Pattern repeats).

Cut out the number of fabric widths required for the curtains.

If more than two widths of fabric are to be used (that is, more than one in each curtain), then the widths will have to be joined together. If three widths are required, then one width should be cut in half, with each curtain being made up of 1½ widths (see Terms and techniques – Joining widths). For unlined curtains, the widths of fabric should be machine sewn together using a flat fell seam (see Terms and techniques) to hide any rough edges.

Step 2

Lay the fabric for one curtain flat and face down. Cut off the selvedges and, using the 4 cm (1½ in) wide card as a guide, fold over side seams of 4 cm (1½ in) down both sides of the fabric. Fold the raw edges under by 1 cm (½ in), press the side seams and pin them down.

Step 3

Trim the bottom edge of the curtain, making sure that the fabric is cut on the grain (see Terms and techniques – Grain) and is level. Then, using the 7.5 cm (3 in) wide card as a guide, fold the fabric over twice to form a double hem, press and pin the hem in place.

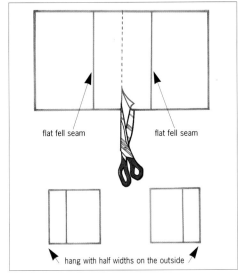

flat fell seam   flat fell seam

hang with half widths on the outside

1

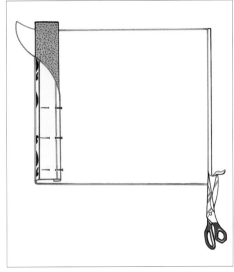

2

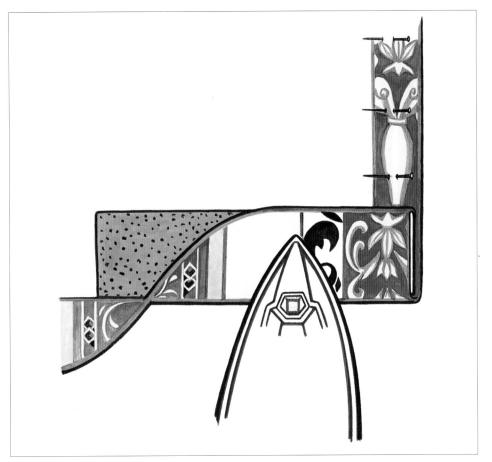

3

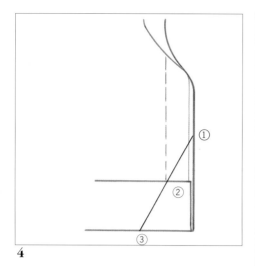

4

Step 4

To make a mitred corner, open up part of the side seam and one fold of part of the hem. Mark three points on a diagonal line: (1) where the doubled hem meets the rough edge of the side seam, (2) where the crease mark of the folded side seam meets the single hem, and (3) where the edge of the folded side seam meets the edge of the single hem. Fold the fabric over along this diagonal line and press. Then fold the side seam and the hem back into place to form a mitre. Do this at each corner.

Step 5

Machine stitch along the top of the fold of both side seams and also along the hem, adjusting the stitch length according to the thickness of the layers of fabric. Remove the pins and hand sew the mitres. Make up the second curtain to the same stage following Steps 1–5.

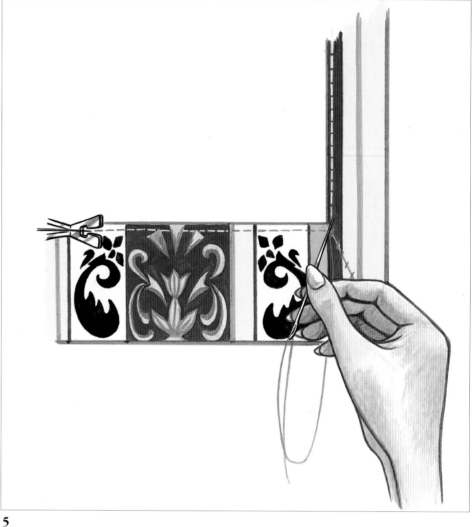

5

Forming ties

Both looped and eyelet headings may be adapted to form ties.
Sew two strips in each loop position along the curtain and simply tie them over the pole or through the rings. They may have long, hanging tails or bows.
Similarly instead of threading a continuous piece of cord through the eyelets, it may be cut in small pieces and tied in bows over the pole.

Day Two

On Day Two, after making up your basic curtains, choose one of the three following heading variations to finish them. Looped, rope and eyelet or taped curtain heading can easily be completed within the day.

Taped heading

Step 1

For taped headings, with the curtain lying face down, measure from the hem and mark the drop measurement at the top of the curtain (plus any allowance made for an 'overlong' curtain). It is at this level that the top of the tape should be sewn. Fold over the excess fabric to form the size of 'frill' you require and cut away any surplus. The tape should then be sewn along both sides, laying it so that the raw edge of the fabric is hidden. Repeat for the second curtain.

Press the curtains and pull the cords of the heading so that each curtain is gathered up and measures 10 cm (4 in) more than half the length of the pole. Knot the cords and tuck the ends under the tape. Hang the curtains.

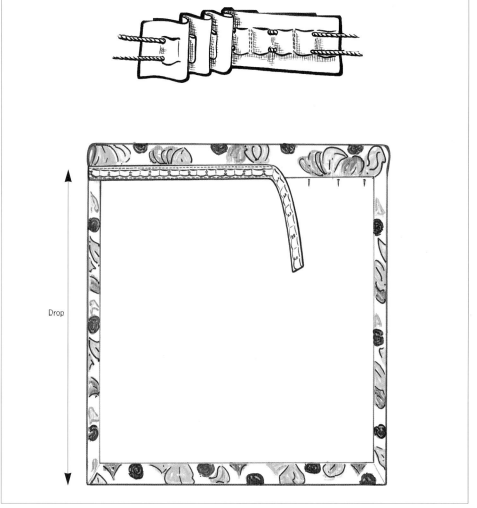

Drop

Using draw rods

If the pole is set high on the wall, curtains with looped and eyelet headings may be difficult to pull. If so, hook a draw rod onto the inside edge of each curtain.

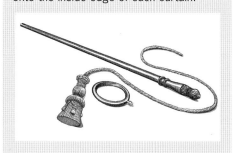

1

Rope and eyelet heading

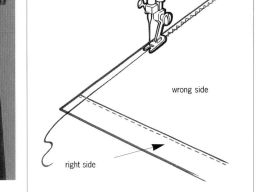

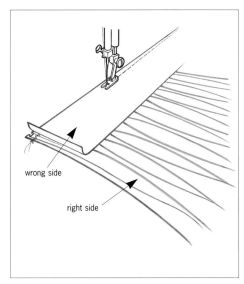

1

2

Step 1

For rope and eyelet headings, gather the top of the curtain by laying a strong thread (e.g. button thread) 1 cm (½ in) from the raw edge and machine sewing a zig-zag stitch over it. Pull this thread to gather the top of the curtain evenly so that it measures half the length of the pole plus 10 cm (4 in).

Step 2

Cut a 15 cm (6 in) wide strip of fabric, measuring the same length as the width of the gathered curtain plus 5 cm (2 in). With right sides together lay this along the top edge of the curtain and machine sew the two together. Trim the raw edges right down before folding over the strip of fabric to cover them.

Step 3

Turn under the raw edge, tidy the ends and pin in place before sewing the strip down along the bottom edge. This strip will now be approximately 6 cm (2½ in) wide. Remove the pins. Fix the eyelets in the centre of the heading strip at 6–10 cm (2½–4 in) intervals. Press the curtain and hang it by threading the rope through the eyelets and over the pole. Repeat the above steps for the second curtain.

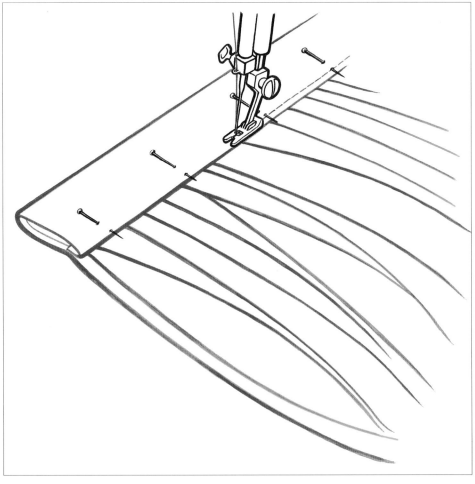

3

Looped heading

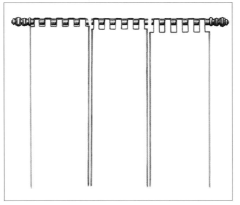

1

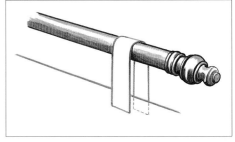

2

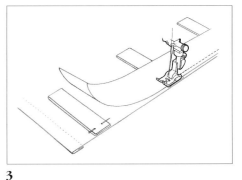

3

Step 1

For looped headings, with the curtain face down, measure from the hem and mark the drop measurement. This may be from the base of the pole or just below it. Draw a line across the curtain at this point, and cut off the excess fabric 2 cm (¾ in) above this line.

Step 2

For the loops, cut strips of fabric approximately 15 cm (6 in) wide. Decide how long the loops are to be and measure around the pole and back to the curtain top. To this measurement, add a 3 cm (1¼ in) seam allowance. Cut out the strips. You will need loops at approximately 15 cm (6 in) intervals across the top of the curtains.

Step 3

With right sides together, fold each strip in half lengthways. Sew down a seam 1.5 cm (⅝ in) from the raw edge. Press the seam open. Turn the strip the right way out and press it again. With the curtain face up, pin the loops to the top, laying them with the raw edges all together. Cut a strip of fabric 7.5 cm (3 in) wide and the length of the curtain width. With right sides together, machine sew this facing to the top of the curtain.

Step 4

Fold over the facing to hide all the raw edges of the tabs and curtain top, then turn the raw edge of the facing under and either machine or hand sew it down. Repeat for the second curtain. Press both curtains, then hang and dress them.

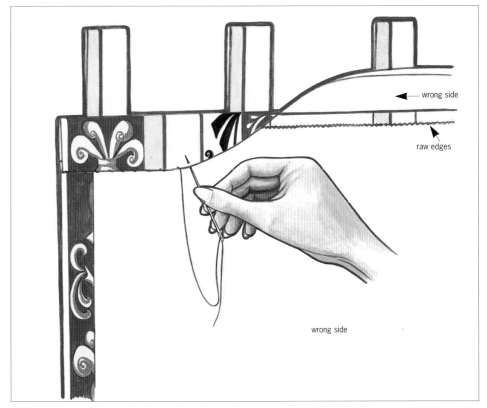

wrong side

raw edges

wrong side

4

Café curtains

These half-curtains have many uses. They can give a room privacy from both inside and out while avoiding the use of a net curtain that may take away too much light.

A café curtain can also hide any unsightly views and can even enhance a distant view by blocking an unattractive foreground. This type of curtain is normally hung across the lower half of a window, either from a tension rod that grips the side walls of the window recess, or from a pole fixed inside or across the recess and attached to the wall.

As these curtains will cover the window both day and night, they need to look good from the back as well as from the front and should therefore be lined (preferably self-lined). The fullness required depends upon the fabric being used, with a firm fabric requiring very little and a fine fabric needing perhaps one and a half times the length of the pole.

When choosing a fabric, find one that looks good both ways up and that has a pattern that will accommodate a cut-out scallop design for a heading; checks and stripes are ideal.

Planning your time

DAY ONE
AM: Put up pole or tension rod, cut out fabric

PM: Make scallop template, draw curtain heading

DAY TWO
AM: Machine sew heading, trim and press curtain

PM: Hand sew sides, hang curtain

Tools and materials

Narrow curtain pole and recess brackets, or tension rod

Hanging rings and clips

Curtain fabric

Matching sewing threads

Card for template

Sewing kit

Sewing machine

Metre ruler and metal tape measure

Soft pencil

Drill, screwdriver etc. for fixing pole

Iron and ironing board

Preparation

Decide on the pole or rod and its position. Measure up for fabric (see below).

Measuring up for fabric

Length of fabric required
Take as the starting point either the base of the rings hanging from the pole, or the top of any attached clips. Measure from here to the window sill (or to a point below if the curtain is to hang outside the recess). Double this measurement and then add on 3 cm (1¼ in) for seam allowances.

Width of fabric required
The curtain should be made with at least a slight fullness – it should not be taut. Measure the length of the pole and add at least 20 cm (8 in). Any pole over one metre in length will need a curtain of more than one width of fabric. Also, the finer the fabric the more the fullness that will be required. The widths will then have to be joined and the pattern matched (see Terms and techniques – Joining widths).

Quantity of fabric required
This will be the length of the curtain (twice the drop, plus 3 cm (1¼ in) for seams), by the number of widths of fabric required (most fabrics are 137 cm (54 in) wide).

Day One
Step 1

Fix the pole or tension rod across the window. Align it with any cross-framing of the window. Cut the length(s) of fabric (see Measuring up, above). If more than one fabric width is required join them together, matching up the pattern (see Terms and techniques – Joining widths). Join the extra fabric to each side to avoid a centre seam.
Fold the fabric in half lengthways with right (that is, patterned) sides together. Pin the fabric together along the top.

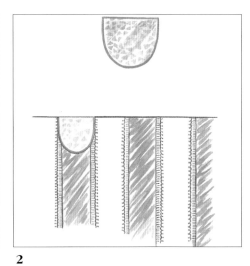

1

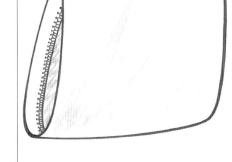

2

Step 2

Cut a piece of card as a template to form the scalloped heading. The finished scallop should be approximately 8 cm (3⅛ in) wide and 10 cm (4 in) deep, but you can alter the size to fit the design of the fabric pattern if required.

Step 3

The curtain rings are attached to tabs approximately 5 cm (2 in) wide, which are fixed between the scallops. Mark the positions for the tabs along the top of the fabric, with an 8 cm (3⅛ in) gap between each drawn scallop to allow for a 1.5 cm (⅝ in) seam allowance. The drawn scallop should be the actual size of the finished article.

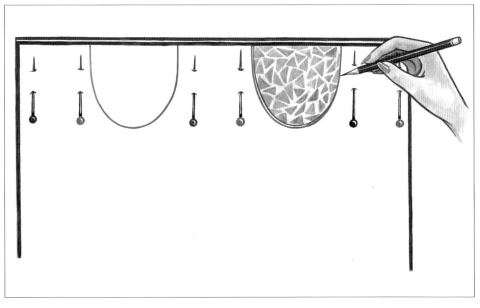

3

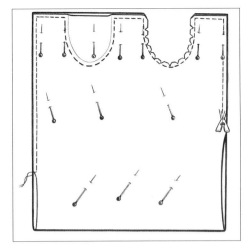

4

Day Two
Step 4

Smooth out the curtain layers and pin them together all over. Beginning on one of the side edges of the curtain, machine sew a line of stitches 1.5 cm (⅝ in) in from the raw edges of the fabric and 1.5 cm (⅝ in) in from the pencil lines marking the scallops. Leave a 20 cm (8 in) opening on the other side of the curtain.

Step 5

Cut out the scallops along the pencil lines and trim off the excess fabric, snipping the seams on the inside of the scallops. Remove the pins and turn the curtain the right side out. Press well, making the corners of the tabs as square as possible. Then hand sew up the side opening using a slip stitch and running the threads between the layers of fabric.

Step 6

Clip or sew a curtain ring to each tab and hang the café curtain.

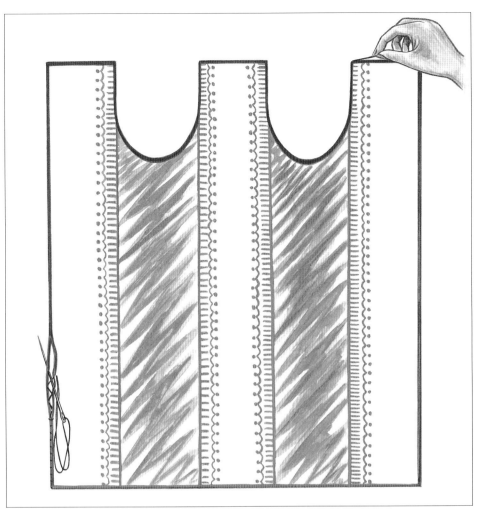

5

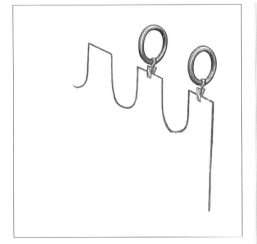

6

Simple café curtain

A very simple café curtain – fixed on one pole across a window recess – can be made by using a cased heading, as described for the dormer curtain on page 36, and sliding the pole through the casing before gathering it slightly. However, the casing will probably have to be wider than 5 cm (2 in) to allow for what is likely to be a thicker pole; allow approximately twice the measurement of the diameter of the pole between the machining lines of the casing.

Soft and flowing 'overlong' curtains

Unlined and machine sewn, these curtains are quick and easy to make. With the extra fabric falling from their headings, they look as though they are hanging beneath a valance.

The flowing lines of these curtains give a room a relaxed and luxurious feel and make them ideal for use in a bedroom. By making them in a soft and fine fabric they will fall easily into folds. A gathering tape sewn to the top of each curtain, but under the valance, provides support for the heading and prevents the 'pull' of the valance exposing the tape.

The curtains can be hung from ring clips or clips attached to rings that grip the top of the heading.

The finished valance heading should be approximately one sixth of the curtain drop.

By making these curtains up with a thick and textured fabric and adding some fringing to the hem of the valance, you can achieve a totally different look; heavy and business-like, they become more suitable for a dining room, study or hall.

Planning your time

DAY ONE

AM: Fix pole above window

PM: Cut out fabric, machine sew all seams and hems

DAY TWO

AM: Design and make curtain heading

PM: Sew on tape, hang curtain

Tools and materials

Curtain fabric

Matching sewing threads

Curtain pole

Curtain rings and/or clips

4–5 m (4½–5½ yd) curtain tape (for example, standard rufflette)

A strip of card 4 cm (1½ in) wide

A strip of card 7.5 cm (3 in) wide

Sewing kit

Sewing machine

Metre ruler and metal tape measure

Iron and ironing board

Drill and screwdriver etc. for fitting the pole to the wall

Preparation

Decide upon the length of the pole and where on the wall it is to be fixed (see page 10).
Measure up for curtain fabric (see below).

Measuring up for fabric
Length of fabric required
Measure from the bottom of the pole to the floor – this is the drop.
To this measurement, add 20 cm (8 in) for hems and turnings and if the curtains are to be 'overlong' add 10–15 cm (4–6 in) more.
Add a further 60–76 cm (24–30 in) to this for the valance heading.

Width of fabric required
See Unlined curtains, page 10.

Quantity of fabric required
Multiply the overall length measurement by the number of widths required: for example, drop plus 20 cm (8 in) (hems and turnings) plus 10–15 cm (4–6 in) (extra length) plus 60–76 cm (24–30 in) (heading) multiplied by two, three or four (widths).
Allowances should be made for the pattern to match (see Terms and techniques – Pattern repeats)

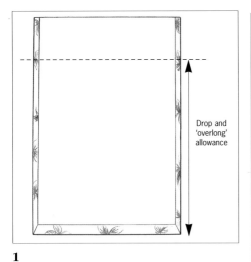

Drop and 'overlong' allowance

1

Day One
Follow Steps 1-5 for Unlined curtains (page 8).

Day Two
Step 1
Then lay the curtain face down and mark the drop measurement (including the 'overlong' allowance) at the top.

Step 2
Fold over the remaining fabric so that the raw edge lies 10 cm (4 in) below this marked line. Turn this raw edge under and pin, then machine sew.

2 x 30–37.5 cm (2 x 1–1¼ ft)

Drop and 'overlong' allowance

2

Step 3

Pin a narrow gathering tape (for example, standard rufflette) to the front of the curtain, with the bottom edge of the tape covering the previous sewing line. Turn the ends of the tape under and machine sew the top and bottom edges of the tape to the front of the curtain.

Step 4

Gather up the tape sufficiently for the curtain to measure half the length of the pole plus approximately 10 cm (4 in). Tie off the cords and hide them between the tape and the fabric.

Step 5

Flop the valance over the front of the curtain, allowing the tape to support the top of the curtain. Repeat Steps 1–5 on the second curtain. Attach the clips to the top of the curtains, press and hang.

To keep the flowing lines of these curtains, arrange them loosely rather than dressing them formally.

Planning the length

Take care not to make these curtains too long or they may take up too much floor space.

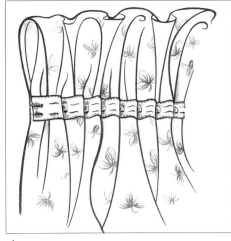

3

4

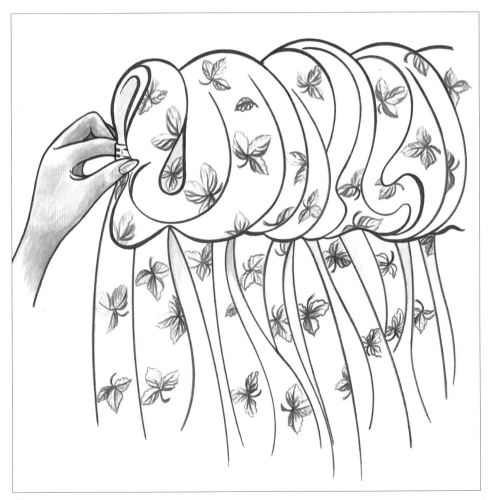

5

Draped curtains I

Draped curtains may be used as the major decorative feature in a small bedroom, or as part of a more complex scheme to dress the windows in a larger room.

This form of window dressing is quick and simple to do and looks very effective, making impact in any situation. The draped curtain is simply one long piece of fabric, literally draped up and over the window. It is kept in place by a number of 'swag creators' that are fixed to the wall above the window. The fabric is formed into rosettes at each end, with simpler gatherings across the window. These curtains are, however, merely decorative, as they do not pull; a simple blind, fitted to pull down over the glass, is therefore necessary for complete privacy (see Roller blind, page 52).

Draped curtains may have tiebacks or holdbacks to complete the design. As they do not pull and are therefore not often handled, the seams may be fixed with an iron-on webbing rather than machine sewn together.

Choose a firm fabric that will stay where it is put, and stand up well when bunched up on the floor. Plain fabrics, stripes and checks are ideal, but as this arrangement is made from one continuous piece of fabric, any pattern does need to be an all-over and random design; that is, one that looks the same when it is hung the right way up, sideways and upside down.

Planning your time

DAY ONE

AM: Fix swag creators to wall, trim fabric

PM: Bond or sew all seams

DAY TWO

AM: Drape fabric and create swags

PM: Arrange curtains, fix holdbacks or tieback hooks to the wall

Tools and materials

8 m (8¾ yd) of furnishing fabric (approximate requirement for an average window)

20 m (22½ yd) of iron-on hemming web OR matching sewing threads

3 or 4 swag creators, valance creators, drape hooks, 'OmKrets' or other similar fitting

7.5 cm (3 in) wide strip of card

4 cm (1½ in) wide strip of card

2 holdbacks, bosses or tieback hooks

Sewing kit

Sewing machine (optional)

Metre ruler and metal tape measure

Iron and ironing board

Drill, screwdriver etc.

Preparation

Measure up for fabric (see below).

Positioning swag creators

The swag creators should be fitted 10–15 cm (4–6 in) above the window recess. The two end ones should be positioned 15 cm (6 in) to the sides of the recess, with the others placed at intervals of approximately 100 cm (39½ in) across the window. Most windows will need a total of three or possibly four swag creators.

Measuring up for fabric

Measure from the floor to above the window recess, across the recess, and down to the floor again. To this measurement add 30 cm (12 in) for hems, 40 cm (15¾ in) for extra draping on the floor, 80 cm (32 in) to form the end rosettes and approximately 15 cm (6 in) extra for each swag.

Keep your measurements generous as it will not matter if there is too much fabric. An average-sized, full-length window, 150 cm (59 in) wide will require approximately 8 m (8¾ yd) of fabric.

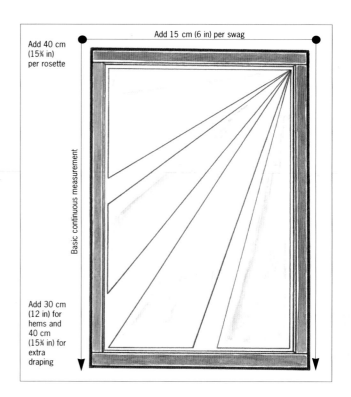

Add 15 cm (6 in) per swag

Add 40 cm (15¾ in) per rosette

Basic continuous measurement

Add 30 cm (12 in) for hems and 40 cm (15¾ in) for extra draping

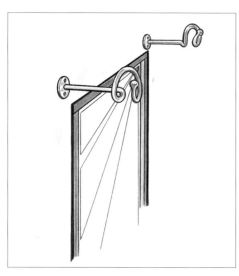

1

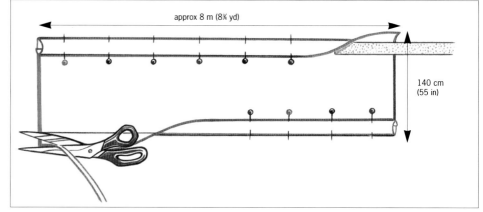

approx 8 m (8¾ yd)

140 cm (55 in)

2

Day One
Step 1

Fix the swag creators to the wall (see above), fitting the corner ones as an opposing pair as shown.

Step 2

Cut the fabric to the required length (see above). Cut off the selvedges (see Terms and techniques) on both sides of

the fabric. Lay the fabric face down and, with the aid of the 4 cm (1½ in) card, fold the side seams over by 4 cm (1½ in), with the raw edges folded under by 1 cm (½ in). Press and pin down.

Step 3

The two ends of the fabric are to be the hems of the curtains, so using the card measuring 7.5 cm (3 in), fold the fabric over twice to form a double hem. Press and pin in place.

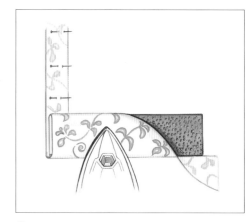

3

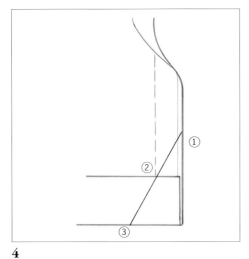

4

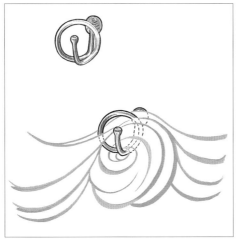

5

6

7

Step 4

For the corners to appear neat and lie flat as they meet the floor, they should each be mitred. To make a mitred corner, open up part of the side seam and one fold of part of the hem. Mark three points on a diagonal line:
(1) where the doubled hem meets the rough edge of the side seam, (2) where the crease mark of the folded side seam meets the single hem, and (3) where the edge of the folded side seam meets the edge of the single hem. Fold the fabric over along this diagonal line and press. Then fold the side seam and the hem back into place to form a mitre. Do this at each corner.

Then either machine stitch along the top of the fold of both side seams and the hem, adjusting the stitch length to allow for the thickness of the fabric layers, and remove the pins; or lay the hemming web on the reverse side of the fabric, between the layers and, following the manufacturer's instructions, press in place. Press a small section together at a time, taking the pins out as you go.

Day Two
Step 5

Press the whole length of fabric. Mark the halfway point between the ends and drape the curtain over the top of the swag creators, matching this point to the centre of the window. Twist one fold of fabric through each of the inside swag creators, pulling the gathered fabric open to cover it.

Step 6

At each corner pull a loop, comprising 40 cm (15¾ in) of fabric, through the circling metal of the side swag creators. Once through, flatten the loops and arrange the fabric to cover all the metalwork and form a rosette shape. Check that both sides are similar.

Step 7

Arrange the swags across the window, folding the outside seams under to give all the edges a well-rounded look. Let the remaining lengths of fabric fall each side of the window and arrange as dress curtains, with the extra fabric bunched evenly on the floor each side. Holdbacks or bosses may be fitted to each side, 10 cm (4 in) outside the window recess (they should be at approximately waist height).

Simple drapes

A less fussy arrangement can be created by just hooking the fabric through each swag creator. Cut a shorter length of fabric for this; too much excess fabric bunched on the floor each side of the window will look out of proportion to the simpler heading.

Draped curtains II

This curtain arrangement is ideal for rooms where the window requires some form of covering both night and day but where a certain amount of daylight is still desired.

Y ou could use this draped window dressing simply for privacy or because the view from a window is uninspiring or ugly and is better hidden. The arrangement is made in three pieces that are sewn together before being fitted directly onto a curtain pole. It is, therefore, very secure. The curtains do not pull back but can be quickly caught back and held in place over a pair of bosses or holdbacks.

Whatever fabric is chosen, whether it is a semi-translucent voile or muslin, or a slightly heavier cotton, silk or calico, it must drape well. The beauty and simplicity of this window dressing is in the soft folds of the fabric; a plain or textured fabric will be most effective. Voiles may have a slight relief or self-coloured pattern.

Where the window is only small, set the pole high above the window recess as this will allow the maximum possible amount of light into the room; the centre draping will then cover only the wall and not too much of the glass.

Preparation

Decide on the fixing point for the curtain pole and on its length (see below). Measure up for the fabric (see below).

Measuring for curtain pole

This pole should be fairly robust and have a diameter of at least 3 cm (1¼ in). The curtain pole itself should extend beyond the window by at least 10 cm (4 in) on each side, with the finials adding to this measurement.

Positioning the pole

The fixing height of the pole will depend on how much of the centre drape is to hang over the glass. The centre drape should, at its deepest point, hang approximately 40 cm (15¾ in) below the pole.

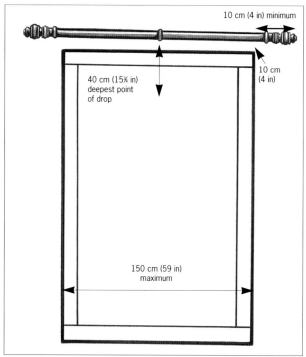

Measuring up for fabric

For each curtain, measure from the pole fixing point to the floor. Add 20 cm (8 in) for extra length, 15 cm (6 in) for the hem and 20 cm (8 in) to cover the pole. If the curtain pole is 160 cm (63 in) long or less, only one width of fabric will be required for each curtain but if the pole is any longer then you will need to add one more width (half a width to each curtain) to obtain an acceptable fullness. This window treatment is not suitable for a wide window.

For the centre drape, hold a measuring tape from one proposed end of the pole to the other, allowing the tape to drape in the middle to approximately 40 cm (15¾ in) below the proposed pole height. Read off this measurement and add it to the amount of fabric required for the two curtains to give you the total amount of fabric required.

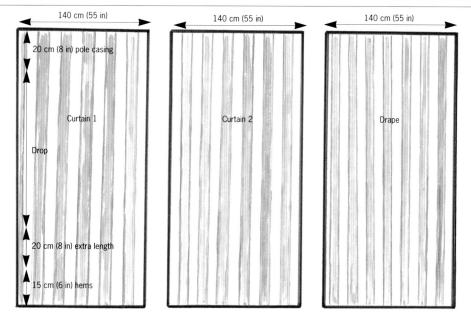

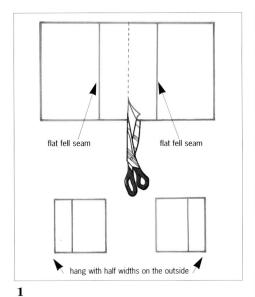

1

Day One
Step 1

Put up the pole brackets (but not the curtain pole) (see page 30). Cut the two curtain lengths by measuring from the pole to the floor and adding 20 cm (8 in) for extra length, 15 cm (6 in) for the hem and approximately 20 cm (8 in) for the pole casing (see page 30). If using a patterned voile, make sure that the lengths match (see Terms and techniques – Pattern repeats).

Cut out the number of fabric widths required. If more than two widths of fabric are to be used (that is, more than one in each curtain), then the widths will have to be joined together. If three widths are required, then one width should be cut in half, with each curtain being made up of 1½ widths (see Terms and techniques – Joining widths).

For unlined curtains, the widths of fabric should be machine sewn together using a flat fell seam (see Terms and techniques) to hide any rough edges.

Step 2

Lay the fabric for one curtain flat and face down. Cut off the selvedges and, using the 4 cm (1½ in) wide card as a guide, fold over side seams of 4 cm (1½ in) down both sides of the fabric.

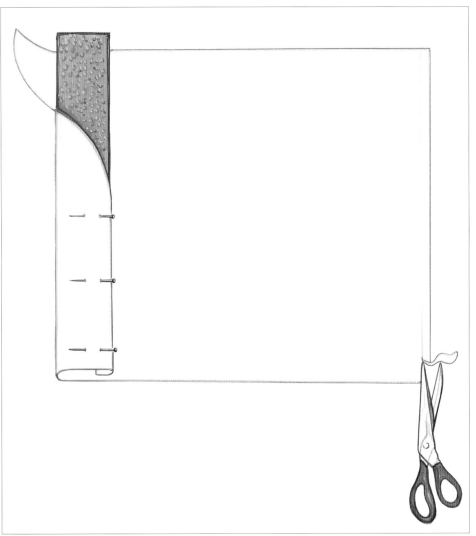

2

Next, fold the raw edges under by 1 cm (½ in), press the side seams and pin them down.

Step 3

Trim the bottom edge of the curtain, making sure that the fabric is cut on the grain (see Terms and techniques – Grain) and is level. Then, using the 7.5 cm (3 in) wide card as a guide, fold the fabric over twice to form a double hem, press and pin the hem in place.

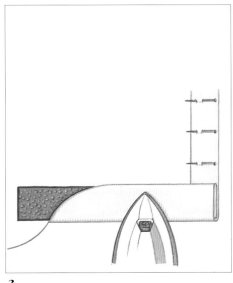

3

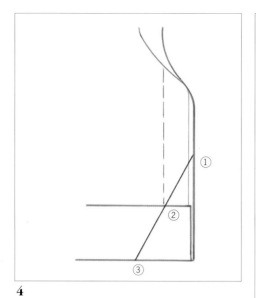

4

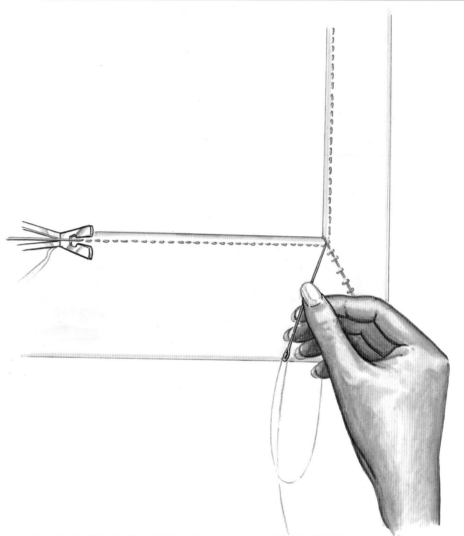

5

Step 4

To make a mitred corner, open up part of the side seam and one fold of part of the hem. Mark three points on a diagonal line: (1) where the doubled hem meets the rough edge of the side seam, (2) where the crease mark of the folded side seam meets the single hem, and (3) where the edge of the folded side seam meets the edge of the single hem. Fold the fabric over along this diagonal line and press. Then fold the side seam and the hem back into place to form a mitre. Pin in place. Do this at each corner.

Step 5

Machine stitch along the top of the fold of both side seams and also along the hem, adjusting the stitch length according to the thickness of the layers of fabric. Remove the pins and hand sew the mitres. Make up the second curtain to the same stage following Steps 1–5.

Day Two
Step 6

Cut the fabric for the centre drape (see page 30). Then cut this piece of fabric into a cropped pyramid shape. Follow Step 7 for how to do this but see illustration 6 for the shape you are aiming for. The length of the fabric is the bottom edge of the draping and the base of the pyramid (A). The top edge of the draping is the top of the pyramid (B) and should measure 50 cm (19¾ in) in length. The angled sides (C) should each measure the same as the width of each curtain.

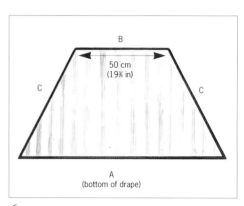

6

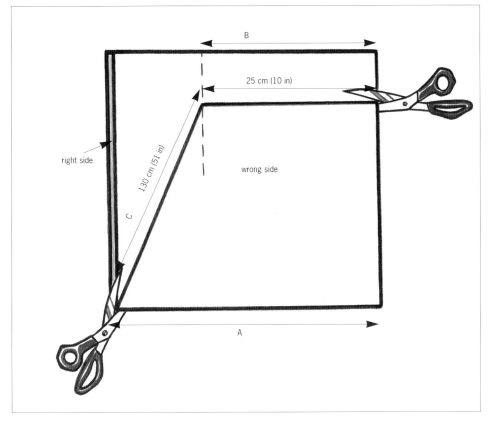

7

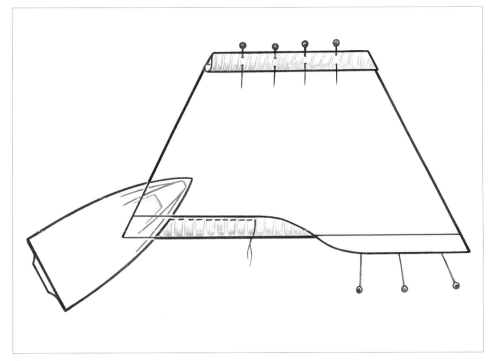

8

Step 7

To cut the pyramid shape, lay the fabric face up and fold it in half lengthways – the right sides of the fabric should now be lying together. From the top edge (B) and 25 cm (10 in) in from the fold, draw a dotted line down towards the base. Now, with the width measurement of one curtain – approximately 130 cm (51 in) – marked out on a metal tape, draw a diagonal line of this measurement from the open ends of the base towards a point on this dotted line. Draw a further line from the point where the diagonal line meets the dotted line towards the folded edge and parallel to the top edge. Cut along these lines.

Step 8

With the wrong side of the fabric face up, turn in a 1.5 cm (⅝ in) hem on both the top and bottom edges of the draping and tuck under. Press, pin and machine sew these hems, then remove the pins.

Step 9

Now attach the tops of the curtains to each side of the centre piece.

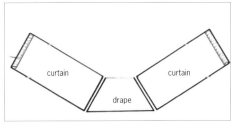

9

Step 10

Lay one curtain right side up, with the centre piece also right side up on top of it. Pin the two pieces together and machine stitch 1.5 cm (⅝ in) from the raw edges. Remove the pins and press the hem towards the curtain. Attach the other curtain to the other side of the centre piece in the same way.

Step 11

Now form the casings at the top of each curtain to hold the pole. Measure around the pole and take a generous measurement; for example, 20 cm (8 in) for a 3.5 cm (1½ in) diameter pole.

Step 12

Fold the top of the curtain down by half this measurement, pin in place and machine stitch a casing to hold the pole. Stitch along the very edge of the fold, then remove the pins.
Make a similar casing at the top of the other curtain.

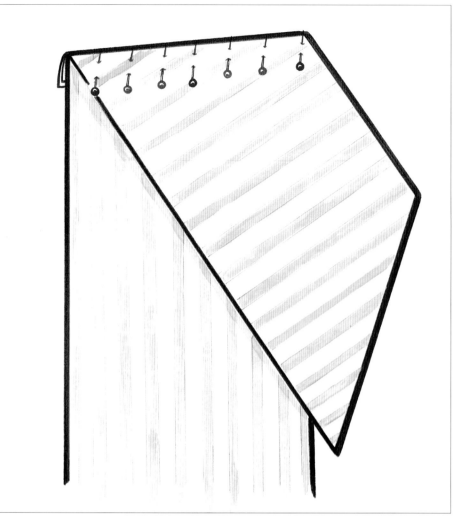

10

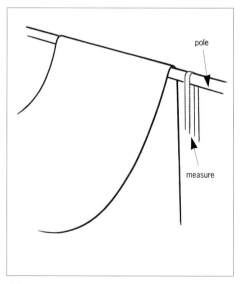

11

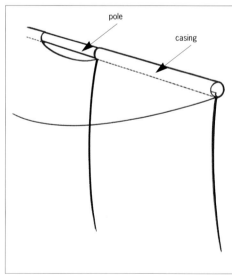

12

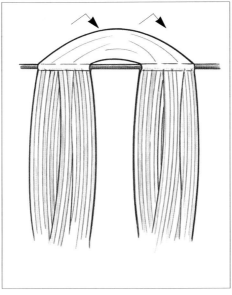

13

Step 13

Press the curtains and draping before sliding the pole through the casings on each curtain.

Step 14

Fix the pole into the brackets and fit the finials to each end. Arrange the gathering of the curtains evenly and then flop the draping over the top of the pole to fall over the curtains. Arrange the centre draping with the base hem folded underneath.

Fix the bosses or holdbacks to the wall at the chosen height, and 10 cm (4 in) outside the window recess. Arrange the curtains and catch them back over these.

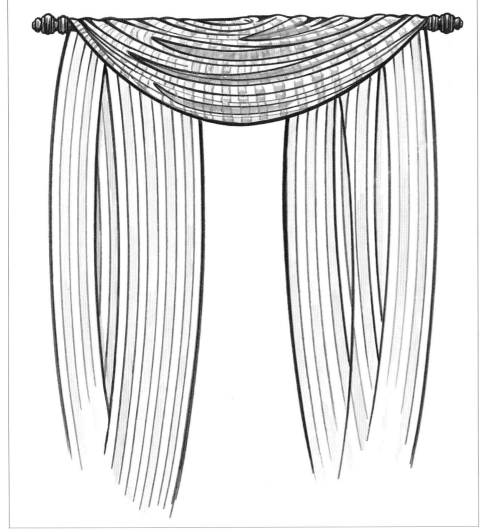

14

Machine sewing fine fabrics

If machine sewing very fine fabrics such as voiles proves difficult and the fabric catches and puckers up, place a sheet of paper beneath the fabric. Sew through this and the fabric, then carefully tear the paper off the back.

Self-lined and caught-back curtains

The ideal way to dress a dormer window is to hang simple frilled curtains from dormer rods. The curtains here are made up using two main fabrics.

S itting high in the roofs of houses, dormer windows look very attractive from the outside. Inside, however, while they make an interesting feature to what is sometimes a rather small room, they are quite difficult to dress. The main reason for this is that they rarely have any wall space around them to fix and hang curtains from. Curtains fitted in the usual way and hung from a rail or pole will cover most of the glass and consequently block out most of the light.

The curtain rods used here are attached to hinged brackets that allow the rods carrying the curtains to be swung across the window at night and to be pushed back against the wall during the day. The curtains are made up using two main fabrics, rather than one with a lining, because both sides will be visible from the room at some time during the day or night. By sewing a frill to three sides of each curtain, and gathering the cased heading at the top, the fabric is allowed to hug the walls and completely fill the space in the dormer.

Planning your time

DAY ONE
AM: Cut dormer rods to correct length, fix dormer brackets to wall; cut out fabrics

PM: Make up frill

DAY TWO
AM: Sew curtain lengths and frill together

PM: Sew cased heading, gather curtains onto rods and fix in place; fix holdbacks to wall

Tools and materials

Front fabric

Back fabric

150 cm (59 in) fabric for frilling

Matching sewing threads

Button twine

One pair of hinged dormer rods

One pair of shallow holdbacks or bosses (or door knobs)

Sewing kit

Sewing machine

Metre ruler and metal tape measure

Soft pencil

Iron and ironing board

Drill, screwdriver etc. for fixing brackets

Preparation

Decide the fixing positions and lengths for the dormer rods (see below). Measure up for fabrics (see below).

Measuring up for dormer rods

Measure the width of the window and buy a pair of dormer rods each measuring at least half the window width.

The brackets attached to these rods are fixed to the wall beside and above the window frame. The rods should cross the window just above the glass, allowing the frill on top of the curtain to cover the window frame and touch the ceiling. The rods should then be cut to such a length that when the curtains are closed across the window, they just meet in the middle.

Measuring up for fabric

Width of fabric required

A width of fabric measuring a maximum of twice the length of the dormer rod is required for each curtain. Few dormer windows will require more than one fabric width per curtain and some will only need a half width on each rod.

Length of fabric required

Measure from the top of the rod to the bottom of the window frame but just above the sill (the frill will fill this space). If two widths of fabric are to be used, the pattern must match across the window (see Terms and techniques – Pattern repeats).

Four pieces of fabric of the same pattern or in two different colours and/or patterns should be cut to these measurements, adding 10 cm (4 in) to the length for the casing and seam allowances and allowing 3 cm (1¼ in) in the width for the side seam allowances. An extra 150 cm (59 in) of one of the fabrics or of a contrasting fabric will be required for the frilling on the curtains.

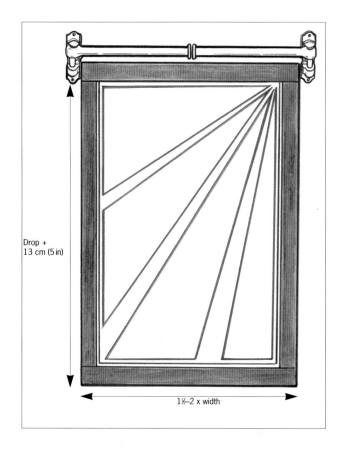

Drop + 13 cm (5 in)

1½–2 x width

Day One
Step 1

Cut the dormer rods to the correct length and fix dormer brackets to the wall. Cut four pieces of curtain fabric, two contrasting pieces for each curtain (see Measuring up for fabric, above). To make the frill, join strips of fabric together to measure twice the length of the seams it is to cover; that is, both side seams and the bottom edge of each curtain. Add these measurements up for both curtains and double it. Strips of fabric joined to measure this length and then gathered will make up to sufficient frilling for both curtains. To cut the fabric for the frill, lay the 150 cm (59 in) length of fabric flat and face down. Draw a series of lines across the fabric at 12 cm (4¾ in) intervals, then cut the required number of strips

137 cm (54 in)

12 cm (4¾ in)

12 cm (4¾ in)

12 cm (4¾ in)

12 cm (4¾ in)

12 cm (4¾ in)

1

and machine sew them together until the correct length is reached. A 12 cm (4¾ in) strip, when folded horizontally and inserted into the seam of the curtain, will produce a frill of 4.5–5 cm (1¾–2 in) in width. If a wider frill is required, cut the strips' widths accordingly (always allowing 3 cm (1¼ in) for seams).

Cut the long strip into two equal lengths, one for each curtain. Mark the halfway point in the length of each new strip with a pin and fold each in half widthways.

Set the sewing machine to a zig-zag stitch and run the stitch over a length of button twine (or similar) in a line 1 cm (½ in) from the raw edges of both strips (see Unlined curtains, Step 1, page 14).

Gather each strip up by pulling the button twine from each end, gathering evenly until each is the same length as the two sides and bottom edge of the curtain fabric. Check that the pin set at the halfway mark is still at the halfway point. Fasten the button twine by winding each end around a pin.

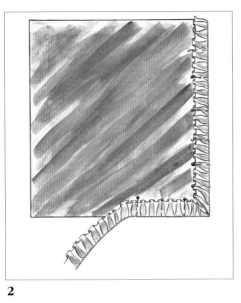

2

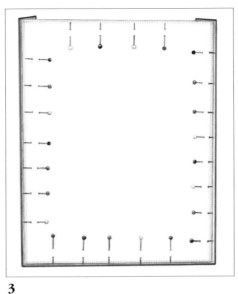

3

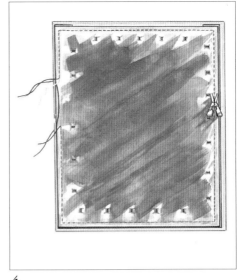

4

Day Two
Step 2

Lay one piece of the darker of the two fabrics face up and mark the centre of the bottom edge. Now lay the frill around the two sides and the bottom edge, and attach the frill at both ends, making sure that the centre markings meet. Pin the frill down with all the raw edges lying together and the fold of the frill on top of the fabric lying towards the middle. Round the corners slightly and put in plenty of pins to hold the excess fabric of the frill away from the seam line. Machine sew the frill to the top fabric along a line 1.5 cm (⅝ in) from the edge and just on the fold side of the zig-zag stitch. Remove the pins except those keeping the corners flat.

Step 3

Again lay this fabric flat with the frill still turned in and then lay the second fabric over the top, pinning it edge to edge all around. Turn the curtain over and machine sew the layers together, taking care to follow the previous sewing line. This time sew along the top as well but leave a 15–20 cm (6–8 in) gap on what will be the outside edge of the curtain. Remove the pins.

Step 4

Turn the curtain right side out, pull the frill into place and press the whole curtain. Hand sew up the opening. Smooth out the top of the curtain and pin it all over to keep the two layers together evenly. Draw two pencil lines across the top, one 5 cm (2 in) from the top and another 5 cm (2 in) below this. Thread the sewing machine with the correct combination of threads (see Terms and techniques – Checking tension) and sew along these lines. These will form the casing for the curtain rods. Unpick the stitching at each end of the casing to allow the rod to slide in. Secure the stitches either side of the casing. Complete the second curtain following Steps 2–4.

Step 5

Remove the end stop and any unwanted rings on the dormer rods and thread the rods through the casing of each curtain. Make sure that each curtain is facing the right way. Screw back the end stops on the rods and hand sew through these to the top edge of the curtain. This will prevent the casing sliding off the end of the rod. Organize the gathering evenly along the rods, to allow what is now a frill on the top of the curtain to stand

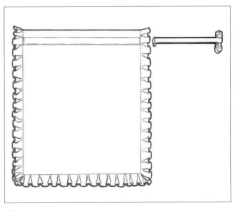

5

up straight. Dress the curtains. Swing the curtains open with the rods against the side walls. Where the curtains hang over the slope of the wall catch them back and mark the wall for the position of the holdback. Fix the holdbacks to the side walls. If the dormer is narrow and the curtains are not very full, small door knobs will probably be sufficient to keep the curtains in position.

Interlined door curtain

Here a heavy interlined curtain is hung across a hall door to make an attractive entrance, but an equally effective result can be obtained across a balcony or terrace door.

H anging a curtain across a hall door will achieve two main purposes. First, there is an instant decorative effect upon what might otherwise have been an uninteresting space; and, second, it will help to keep the hall warm.

By using a thick main fabric, as well as interlining and lining and by making it drape right to the floor, this curtain becomes an effective barrier against draughts. In this case, a synthetic interlining is preferable to the traditional cotton 'bump' as it is much easier to work with and is almost as thick. Adding some fringing or braid to the curtain edge will give a more exotic look if so desired.

A pole should be fixed over the doorway, either on the wall above or from the ceiling. It needs to extend sufficiently to one side of the door or the other, to allow the curtain to be pulled back, clear of the opening door. If this is not possible, the curtain will need to be hung from the door itself. A portière rod can be fixed to the back of the door and this will rise as the door is opened, lifting the curtain clear of the floor and the opening door.

If the back of the curtain can be seen from the outside, choose a coloured fabric as a lining. A plain glaze chintz will be more colourfast than a coloured sateen lining fabric.

Planning your time

DAY ONE
AM: Fix pole above or on the door

PM: Cut out fabrics; hand sew main fabric and interlining

DAY TWO
AM: Hem lining and hand sew to curtain

PM: Machine sew heading tape onto curtain; hand sew braid to curtain edge; hang curtain

Tools and materials

Curtain fabric

Synthetic interlining

Curtain lining

Matching sewing threads

Pencil pleat tape (150 cm [59 in] per fabric width)

Plastic curtain hooks

2.5 m (2¾ yd) fringing or braid

Curtain pole and rings or portière rod

A strip of card 4 cm (1½ in) wide

A strip of card 7.5 cm (3 in) wide

Sewing kit

Sewing machine

Metre ruler and metal tape measure

Drill and screwdriver etc. for fitting pole

Iron and ironing board

Preparation

Measure up for curtain pole or portière rod (see page 10).
Measure up for fabrics (see below).

Measuring up for fabrics

One width of fabric gathered up with a length of heading tape will
be quite wide enough for most doors.

To find the length of fabric needed, measure from the base of the
rings on the pole to the floor and add approximately 15 cm (6 in) to
allow the curtain to drape on the floor – this is the curtain drop.
To this measurement you should add a further 20 cm (8 in) for
hems and turnings.

Interlining and lining of the same length will also be required (see
Terms and techniques – Linings and interlinings).

Day One
Step 1

Put up the curtain pole or portière rod.
Cut out the main fabric (see above) and
trim off the selvedges from both sides.
Lay the fabric face down on a large
table. Cut the interlining to the same
length and place it on top of the main
fabric, smoothing it out and trimming it
to exactly the same size. The two
fabrics will cling together and should
now be treated as one.

Draw a pencil line down the full
length of each side, 4 cm (1½ in) in
from the raw edges. Using the lines as a
guide, hand sew these two layers
together using a large back stitch,
catching just a few threads of the main
fabric on each stitch.

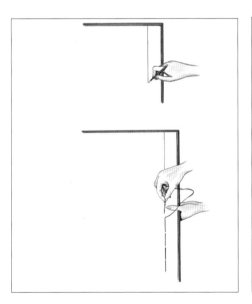

1

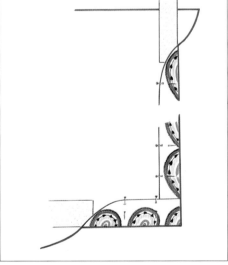

2

Step 2

Using the strips of card as guides, fold
the side seams in by 4 cm (1½ in) and
then fold up a double hem of 7.5 cm
(3 in) plus 7.5 cm (3 in). Pin the side
seams, hem in place and mitre the two
corners (see Step 3).

Step 3

To mitre each of the corners, open up the bottom of the side seams and the side edges of the hem by one layer. Mark a diagonal line across each of the corners by joining three points: the first on the bottom of the hem 8 cm (3⅛ in) from the raw edge of the side seam, the second on the top of the single hem 4 cm (1½ in) in from the side edge, and the third on the raw edge of the side seam 7.5 cm (3 in) above the fold of the single hem. Fold the fabric on these lines, press and then fold the corners of the hem back up and the side seams back in to form a mitre at each corner.

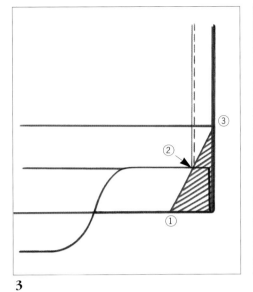

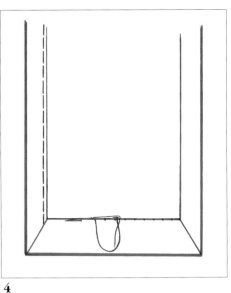

3

4

Step 4

Hand sew the side seams by using a large back stitch, sewn 3 cm (1¼ in) in from the curtain edge. Sew along the hem by using a fairly loose hemming stitch, running the needle through the layers, hiding the threads and catching only a thread or two of the main fabric. Close the mitres by sewing the edges with a ladder stitch (see Terms and techniques – Ladder stitch).

Day Two
Step 5

Cut the length of lining and, with the aid of the wider card, fold up a double hem of 7.5 cm (3 in) plus 7.5 cm (3 in). Pin in place and machine sew along the top edge of the hem. The slightly shinier side is the right side of the fabric. Lay the lining face up over the back of the curtain. Starting from the middle of the curtain, pin the hem of the lining along a line 5 cm (2 in) above the hem of the curtain. Smooth out the lining towards the sides, folding under or trimming off the excess lining fabric and pinning the lining to the side seams. It should meet the mitre seam and lie approximately 2.5 cm (1 in) from the sides of the curtain. Slip stitch the sides of the lining, again hiding the threads in the layers of fabric. Remove the pins from the sides but not the hem.

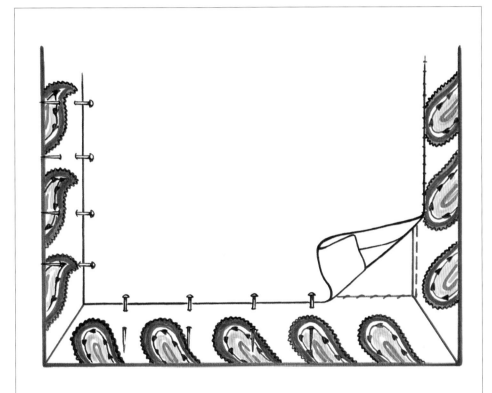

5

Step 6

With the curtain lying face down, smooth out the lining and fix a row of pins approximately 20 cm (8 in) from the top of the curtain. Fold over approximately 5 cm (2 in) of the top raw edges of the main fabric, interlining and lining.

Step 7

Pin the length of pencil pleat tape 1 cm (½ in) below the folded edge. Fold under the ends of the tape, making sure you release the cords, and machine sew the tape to the top of the curtain along both edges of the tape.

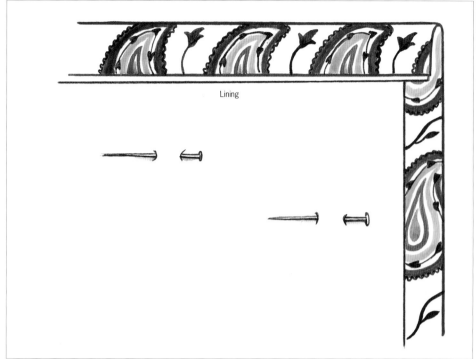

Lining

6

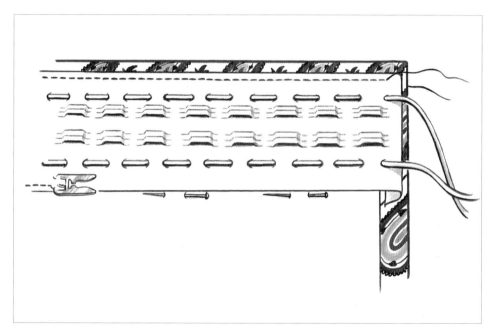

7

Step 8

Remove all pins. Press the curtain, taking care to keep the edges rounded rather than sharp. Pull up the cords in the tape, gathering the curtain to fit the pole. Knot the cords and roll up the excess, pushing it between the tape and the fabric.

Step 9

Hand sew any fringing or braid to the leading edge of the curtain. Glue or oversew the two cut edges to prevent the fringe from fraying. Insert the plastic hooks at intervals of approximately 15 cm (6 in) across the tape and hang the curtains. Dress them by arranging the folds down the length of the curtain.

If you wish, you could always add a tieback or holdback at a later date.

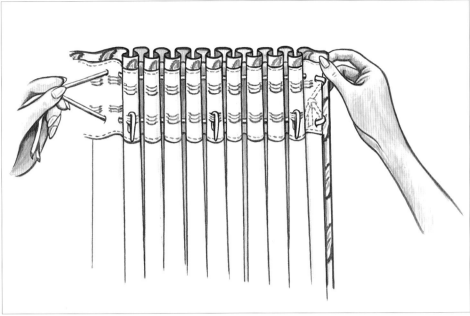

8

9

Making traditional curtains

This single width interlined door curtain is the prototype for all traditionally made curtains. Join widths of fabric together (matching up the pattern), to make a pair of curtains to fit any sized window. However, it will take longer than one weekend to make a pair of curtains!

Swags and tails

While this draped pelmet can be fitted over a curtain, it looks particularly good over a window that really needs no curtain but would be softened by some form of decoration.

The term 'swags and tails' conjures up a rather elaborate image of vast folds of fabric draped in scallops across a window, with heavily fringed tails hanging at each side. They can, however, be made quite simply, using a long panel of fabric and either 'throwing' it over a pole or attaching it to a pelmet board. If the fabric has a tendency to slip, staple or tack it to the underside of the pole.

By adapting the basic methods described here, several different styles may be achieved. For instance, the longer the fabric panel is made, the further down the window the tails will hang. The ends of the tails may be left straight or may be curved for a pointed effect.

Choose the fabric carefully; this is where that beautiful piece of material bought for its dramatic effect that has never quite found a suitable home will come into its own. If the fabric is patterned, centralize the main feature and, if necessary, add further widths to each side. With no pattern to look odd hanging upside down, plain fabrics, stripes and checks may be cut from the length of the fabric. Unless the panel is made from a voile or similar fabric, it should be lined and, if possible, interlined. If the window dressing is to have long, curved tails then the panel should be self-lined or lined with a contrasting fabric, as the back of the panel will show when the tails fall in folds to the sides of the window.

Another method of making attractive swags is shown on page 49. Here decorative cords are tied in bows to produce the swags. A vast range of cords is available and allows endless colour combinations.

Planning your time

DAY ONE
AM: Fix pole above window or make up pelmet board, finalize design ideas

PM: Cut out fabrics

DAY TWO
AM: Sew fabric layers together

PM: Staple panel to board, arrange fabric and tie cording in place or attach tapes to back of panel; throw panel over pole and tie in place

Tools and materials

Main fabric

Lining fabric (see main text)

Interlining or wadding (if required)

Matching sewing threads

Decorative cord (approximately 100 cm [39½ in])

50 cm (19¾ in) tape

Covered pelmet board (a 5 x 2 cm [2 x ¾ in] length of timber cut to the span measurement) and sufficient angle brackets or curtain pole and fittings

Sewing kit

Large pair of scissors

Sewing machine

Metre ruler and metal tape measure

Soft pencil

Iron and ironing board

Tacks and hammer, or staples and staple gun

Drill, screwdriver etc. for fitting board or pole

Preparation

Decide whether the panel is to hang from a narrow pelmet board or a pole (see below). Measure up for fabrics (see below).

Measuring up for pelmet board or pole

The board or pole should be fitted approximately 10 cm (4 in) above the window recess and extend beyond the recess by approximately 10–15 cm (4–6 in) on each side.

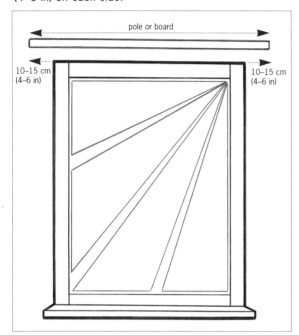

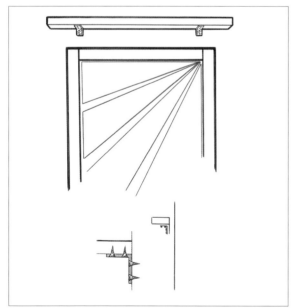

Fixing the pelmet board or pole

Fix the pole above the window recess or cut the length of timber to the correct measurement, cover it with a lining fabric and attach the angle brackets. Mark the fixing points onto the wall.

Measuring up for fabrics

Width of fabric required

To create a swag with a 50 cm (19¾ in) drop, a width of fabric measuring 70 cm (27½ in) is required. If the span of the proposed swag is more than 150 cm (59 in), then an even wider panel of fabric will be needed for the 50 cm (19¾ in) drop.

Length of fabric required

To the span measurement (that is, the length of the pole or the pelmet board) add 10 cm (4 in) to each side for 'take up' plus the lengths of the two tails or side pieces.

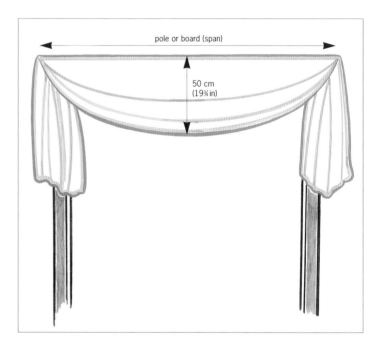

The panel should be made up by cutting pieces from the width of the fabric or by using one continuous piece cut from the length. If the pelmet is self-lined it will be particularly economical to cut the fabric lengthways.

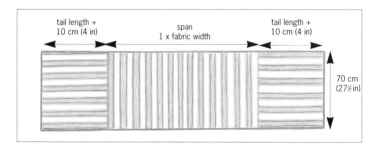

Three pieces of fabric are required, cut to the above measurements: the main fabric, the lining and, if possible, the interlining or wadding. Cut all the pieces to exactly the same size, with an extra 1.5 cm (⅝ in) seam allowance all around.

Draped 'pelmet' with decorative cording

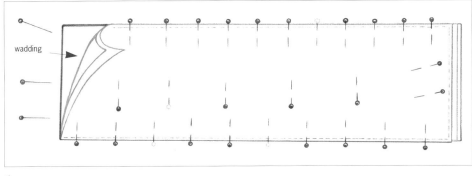

1

2

Day One
Step 1

Take the length measurement of the
board and add 10 cm (4 in) to each side
for fabric 'take up', and then a further
15 cm (6 in) on each side. If this
measurement is less than 140 cm
(55 in), cut one width of fabric 70 cm
(27½ in) deep; if it is more, cut two,
taking the pattern repeat into
consideration (see Terms and
techniques – Pattern repeats). There
should be an extra 1.5 cm (⅝ in) seam
allowance all around.

If two widths of fabric are to be used,
join the widths together, matching the
pattern and avoiding a central seam by
placing half widths at each side.

Cut out the lining and interlining or
wadding to the same size. Adding a
layer of wadding of some sort will
make the folds on this draping much
softer and more rounded but it is not
absolutely necesssary.

If wadding is to be used, lay it flat and
then lay the main fabric, right side up,
on top, carefully smoothing out all the
creases. Now lay the lining right side
down on top of this, again smoothing
out any creases. Pin together the layers
of fabric.

Day Two
Step 2

Machine sew the fabric layers together,
1.5 cm (⅝ in) from the raw edges,
leaving a 30 cm (12 in) gap along the
top edge. Remove the pins and trim
the corners. Turn the panel right side
out and press well, taking care to keep
the lining hidden from the front.
Hand sew up the opening on the top
edge. For a curtain pole hanging go to
page 51.

For a pelmet board hanging, mark the
centre of the panel and the centre of
the board, then staple the centre of the
top edge of the panel to that of the top
surface of the board. Continue stapling
the panel to the board until both ends
are reached. Allow the fabric to drape
over the edge of the board.

Step 3

Lay the board and fabric panel on a flat surface with the fabric face up. Lay a 50 cm (19¾ in) length of decorative cord at each end of the board, under the fabric.

Step 4

Gather the fabric up from the base of the panel at each end of the board and tie the cord ends together into a bow. Shape the folds into the swag and arrange the ends. Screw the angle brackets attached to the board into the marked holes on the wall. Readjust the folds in the swag, and the hanging of the draping generally.

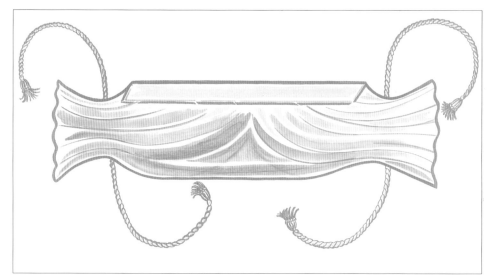

3

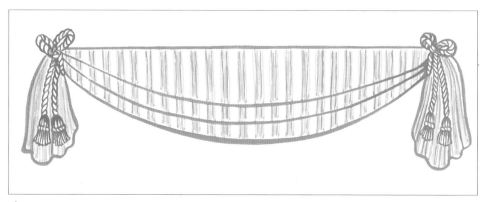

4

Joining patterned fabric

If the fabric pattern is such that the window dressing would look better with the pattern hanging the same way up on the tails as on the swag, then the basic panel should be made up by joining together three pieces of the fabric rather than cutting it in one long strip. Cut a width of fabric 70 cm (27½ in) deep to the proposed width of the swag and the 'take up' allowances. Cut a further length of fabric to the measurement of the drop of the tails, and cut this into two 70 cm (27½ in) strips. Attach these strips by their top edges to the sides of the centre width fabric that is to form the swag. Press the seams open. Sewing the fabric together in this arrangement will allow the pattern in each tail to fall the right way up (see page 48).

Self-lined with long tails over a pole

Day One
Step 1

Decide on the length of the tails (80 cm [32 in] is a good length for an average-sized window; that is, two thirds of the span). To these measurements add the length of the pole, plus 10 cm (4 in) each side for 'take up'. If the drop of the swag is to be 50 cm (19¾ in), the width of the fabric should be cut to approximately 70 cm (27½ in). From one width of 137–140 cm (54–55 in) wide main fabric, cut two 70 cm (27½ in) strips (one for the top and one as lining) to the length of the tails, span and 'take up' allowances. If adding a layer of wadding, cut a 70 cm (27½ in) strip to that same length measurement.

Step 2

If wadding is to be used, lay it flat and then lay the main fabric, right side up, on top. Now lay the lining right side down on top of this. Pin the layers of fabric together (see Step 1, page 49). Shape the tails by cutting along diagonal lines drawn from the top corners of the strips towards the bottom edge at the start of the tail measurement. These lines may be straight or curved.

Day Two
Step 3

Machine sew together, 1.5 cm (⅝ in) from the raw edges, leaving a 30 cm (12 in) gap along the top edge. Remove the pins and trim any corners. Turn the panel right side out and press, taking care to keep the lining hidden from the front. Hand sew the opening on the top edge. Lay the fabric panel face down on a flat surface and sew a 50 cm (19¾ in) length of tape 10 cm (4 in) down from the centre of the top edge onto the back of the panel. If the swag is wider than 120 cm (47¼ in), use two or three tapes. With the main fabric facing the room, tie the tapes around the centre of the pole. Drape the two tail ends behind the pole so that they rest against the wall space at each side of the window. Arrange the draping to suit the room and the fabric.

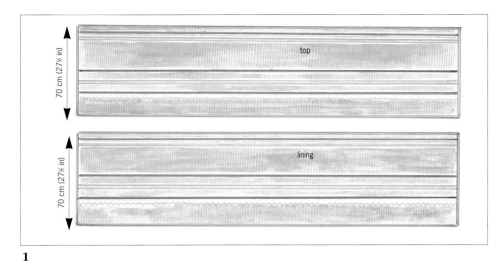

1

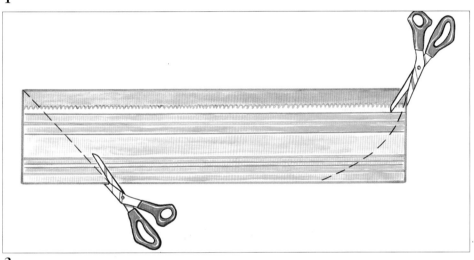

2

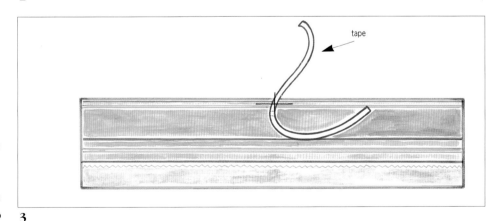

3

Roller blind

This roller blind decorated with a Victorian bathing scene brightens up a bathroom. The design can be adapted to any theme using your own stencil or a ready-made one.

Roller blinds are the most basic form of window dressing – they are merely a length of stiffened fabric attached to a pole – yet they are one of the most useful. As the pole or roller has a spring mechanism a roller blind can cover or uncover a window in an instant. Roller blinds are normally fitted inside a window recess, next to the glass, and are particularly suitable for high windows or those at awkward angles, such as Velux windows, as they are streamlined and very practical.

Roller blinds were originally used to protect the main curtains and other room furnishings from the sun, and were usually made from plain lining fabrics. Today's roller blinds, though, have their own place in window dressing and can be made from most closely woven fabrics that have been stiffened (either by the manufacturer or by the use of a spray or dip). A good fabric to use is soft upholstery calico; this, once washed to remove any dressing, can be painted or stencilled to take up the colours and theme of the room.

The advantages of buying a special blind fabric are that it will not need any extra stiffening, it will not fray and it will be fade-resistant. If, however, you are painting or stencilling your own fabric use a spray stiffener and one that only needs to be sprayed onto the back of the fabric. This leaves the front surface free to take the paint.

Planning your time

DAY ONE

AM: Fix brackets and cut roller to size, cut out fabric

PM: Seam blind; spray blind with fabric stiffener and hang blind to dry

DAY TWO

AM: Stencil or paint blind

PM: Attach blind to roller, fit cord holder

Tools and materials

Fabric (see page 54)

Matching or contrasting sewing threads

Heavy-duty glue (for pre-treated fabrics only)

Roller blind kit

Wooden channels (for Velux windows only)

Spray stiffener (PVA-based)

Fabric paints

Stencils

Spray Hold or Spray Mount

Basic sewing kit

Sewing machine

Metre ruler and metal tape measure

Set square

Soft stencil brushes

Iron and ironing board

Tacks and hammer or staples and staple gun

Drill, screwdriver and small saw

Preparation

Decide where on the window the blind is to hang, either against the glass or outside the recess. Measure up for the fabric and the blind mechanism kit (see below).

Measuring up
For blind mechanism kit
Inside the window recess: measure from one wall to the other.
Outside the recess: allow 4 cm (1½ in) extra on each side of the window recess.
Roof or sloping windows (Velux): measure the length of the slope for the wooden side channels.
The roller should be bought larger than required and cut to fit exactly.

Measuring up for fabrics
Pre-treated and plastic-coated fabrics
Width: As for blind kit.
Length: The drop, plus 35 cm (14 in) to cover the roller and allow for hems.
The drop measurement for a blind sitting outside the recess is from 5 cm (2 in) above the window recess to 5 cm (2 in) below the sill.

Patterned fabrics (see Terms and techniques – Pattern repeats)
Width: As for blind kit plus 7 cm (2¾ in) (approximately)
Length: As for pre-treated fabrics plus enough to position any pattern correctly.

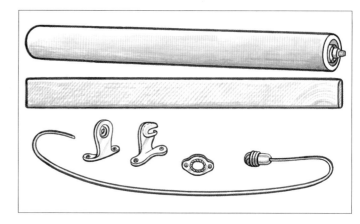

Calico and other plain fabrics to be painted or stencilled
In order for the paints to permeate through the fabric and for the stiffener to be absorbed into the calico, these fabrics should be washed before use to remove all dressings and finishes. Generous allowances should be made for shrinkage. Calico is manufactured in a variety of widths, so check that one width of fabric will be enough.
Width: As for blind kit plus 15 cm (6 in) (approximately).
Length: As for pre-treated fabrics plus shrinkage allowances.

Day One
Step 1

Fix the brackets following the instructions for the roller blind kit. If the blind is to hang inside the recess, fix the brackets as close to the walls as possible. If hanging outside, fix them to the wall 4 cm (1½ in) either side of the recess and at least 5 cm (2 in) above it.

Cut the roller to fit between the brackets. Hammer home the round pin to the end of the roller.

Cut out the fabric following the guidelines above for measuring up. The blind should be made to cover the roller completely, including the metal ends but not the pins.

Step 2

Cut the fabric using a set square for the corners and making very sure to cut along the grain of the fabric (see Terms and techniques – Grain). Lay the fabric face down and turn in the side seams

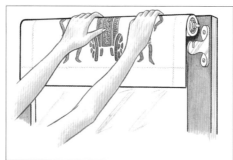

1

(except in the case of pre-treated fabrics, which need no seams). Trim these seams to measure 3 cm (1¼ in) each, remove all loose threads and pin in place.

Using a large zig-zag stitch, machine sew down these side seams, with the stitching covering the raw edges. If you are using a plain fabric, such as calico, you could consider using a thread in a contrasting colour.

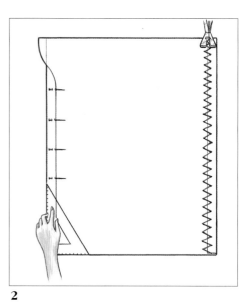

2

Ironing calico

Calico is very difficult to iron, but ironing it wet makes the process easier.

Step 3

Fold over the hem to form a casing wide enough to take the batten. Pin in place and machine stitch as with the side seams. The pre-treated fabrics may be glued into place. Blinds made for Velux windows require a slightly longer batten that will fit into the side runners or notches.

Hang the blind outside and spray the back with the stiffening liquid. Leave to dry at room temperature.

Day Two
Step 4

Lay the blind flat with the right side facing you. Now plan the design for your blind, and position any stencils. Keep all the designs within the seam lines and remember that the top 30 cm (12 in) of the fabric will be covering the roller even when the blind is down. Spray the back of the stencil with Spray Hold or Spray Mount and press it firmly in place. Following the instructions provided with the fabric paints, stencil the design onto the blind. Practise first on a spare piece of fabric, working with a slightly wet brush and not using too much paint. Most fabric paints will dry very quickly.

Attach the fabric to the roller with tacks or staples.

Step 5

Insert the batten into the casing at the bottom of the blind and screw the cord holder in place in the centre. Iron the blind to set the fabric paints. Place the roller between the brackets and, following the instructions on the blind kit, set the tension correctly.

In the case of Velux or other sloping or roof windows, fit wooden side channels or notches to the inside of the recesses to keep the blind against the glass.

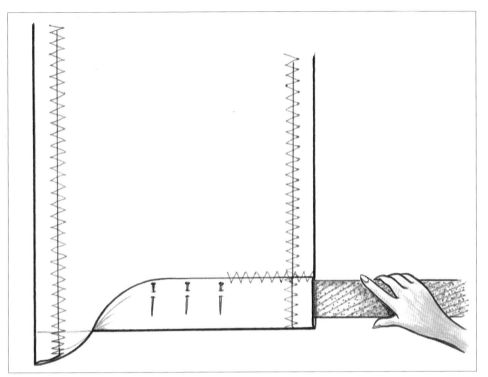

3

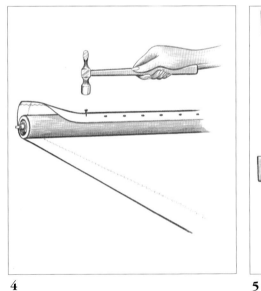

4

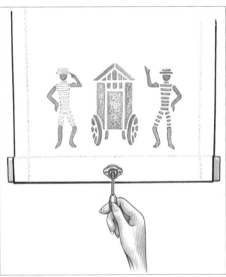

5

Paints for stencilling

While fabric paints are obviously the most suitable to use for decorating fabric, it is possible in theory to use any sort of paint; for example, oil-based spray paints, emulsion, matt or silk, or eggshell. Test the paints on a sample piece of fabric and hold it against the glass to see how much light filters through. Check how thick and how stiff it is once the paint dries, and that the blind rolls up evenly over it. Fabric paints, once ironed, are permanent and are the most translucent.

Pull-up blind

Pull-up blinds have the advantage of taking up very little space. They use only a minimum amount of fabric to cover a window and are simple to make.

As these blinds are pulled up, the fabric folds to form pleats at the top of the window. Unlike Roman blinds, however, there are no wooden poles to support these pleats. They therefore hang with a softer and more relaxed look to them. When hanging down, pull-up blinds are as smooth and uncluttered as Roman blinds. They are not fussy and fit into any room setting, adding interest to a small hall window while being simple enough for a bathroom or cloakroom.

As the pleats of a pull-up blind are unsupported, it is better to reserve them for fairly small windows; if the window is too wide, the pleats can fall out of shape and the blind will just be a mass of creased fabric. The thickness and weight of the fabric you choose for your blind will determine the overall look that you achieve; thicker and stiffer fabric will create firmer and crisper pleats, while a finer fabric will allow the pleats to fall out slightly and give an almost gathered look. Try pleating up any proposed fabric (preferably before you have bought it), moving it about to see how well the fabric stays in place. The ideal fabric for these blinds is a tightly woven medium-weight cotton (see Terms and techniques – Furnishing fabrics). As with all blinds, do be careful when choosing patterned fabrics to centralize any large pattern and position any stripes evenly (see Roman blind – page 60).

Planning your time

DAY ONE

AM: Cut out top fabric and lining, and machine sew together

PM: Hand sew plastic rings to back of blind

DAY TWO

AM: Prepare and position top hanging board

PM: String blind and hang; fix cleat to wall

Tools and materials

Top fabric

Lining fabric

Matching sewing threads

20–30 small plastic rings

Nylon cord (approximately 8–10 times the length of the blind)

5 x 2 cm (2 x ¾ in) wooden batten cut to the same measurement as the width of the blind

Angle brackets and screws to fit batten

Screw eyelets – between 4 and 6

Brass cleat

An acorn or similar to keep cord ends together

Basic sewing kit

Large pair of scissors

Sewing machine

Metre ruler and metal tape measure

Soft pencil

Tailor's chalk

Iron and ironing board

Tacks and hammer or staples and staple gun

Drill, screwdriver, screws and wallplugs

Preparation

Decide on the position of the blind – is it to hang inside the window recess or outside, on the wall or from the ceiling? Measure up for top fabric and lining (see below).

Measuring up for fabrics

Inside the recess: Measure across the window (from wall to wall) for the width and add 3 cm (1¼ in) for seams. Measure from the top of the window to the sill (the 'drop') and add 10–15 cm (4–6 in) for seams and hanging allowance.

Outside the recess: Measure across the window, allowing at least 5 cm (2 in) of overlap onto the wall on each side, plus 3 cm (1¼ in) for seams. Decide on the height of the blind, which should be no more than 15 cm (6 in) above the recess. Measure from this point to the sill if it protrudes, or a minimum of 5 cm (2 in) below if it does not. Add 10–15 cm (4–6 in) to this drop measurement for the seams and hanging allowance.

One width of fabric will be wide enough for all pull-up blinds. The length of fabric needed will be equal to the drop measurement of the proposed blind, plus seam and heading allowances. If choosing a fabric with a large pattern, buy extra fabric so that the pattern can be positioned as you want it (see Terms and techniques – Pattern repeats).

All pull-up blinds look better if they are lined, so choose a tightly woven cotton sateen or a plain-coloured glazed chintz (see Terms and techniques – Linings). You will need the same amount of lining fabric as top fabric.

Day One
Step 1

Cut out the top fabric to the measurements of the window plus the allowances, taking care to cut the fabric accurately along the grain (see Terms and techniques - Grain), centralizing and positioning any pattern. Cut out the lining fabric to exactly the same measurements. Lay the top fabric flat on a table, face up. Lay the lining, face down, on the top. Smooth out all wrinkles and creases from the two fabrics and pin them together, leaving a 1.5 cm (⅝ in) seam allowance. Then machine sew down both sides and along the base. Remove all pins, trim the corners and turn the blind the right way out. Press the blind, taking care to press out the seams.

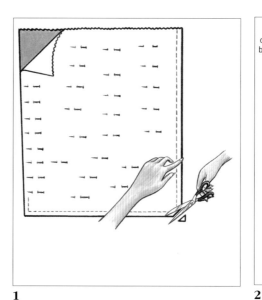

1

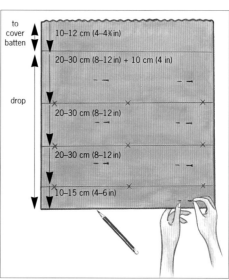

2

Step 2

The next stage is to arrange the pleats. The ideal depth for these pleats is 15 cm (6 in), as pleats of this size should, once trained, fall easily into place each time the blind is pulled up. If you are using a very firm fabric then the pleats may be larger, and, similarly, if the fabric is light and fine then the pleats may be smaller. Lay the blind flat with the lining face up, smooth it out and pin the two layers together all over. Using tailor's chalk or a similar temporary marker pen, measure the drop of the blind and draw a line across it. Then, below this line, mark out the positions for the plastic rings and cords that will be needed to form the pleats. For a pleat of approximately 15 cm (6 in) depth, the spacing between the rings along the length of the blind should be approximately 30 cm (12 in).

There should be an allowance of approximately 10 cm (4 in) (incorporated in the top pleat) at the top of the blind to accommodate the screw eyes and the cording system. The rest of the blind should be divided equally into sections of approximately 30 cm (12 in), while allowing for a half pleat of 15 cm (6 in) at the base. Draw lines across the blind at these points.

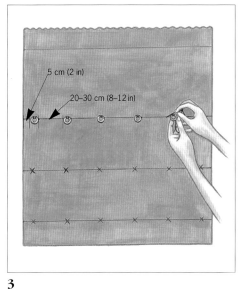

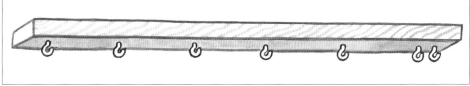

4

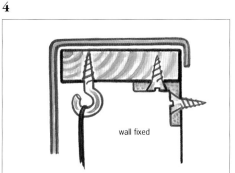

wall fixed

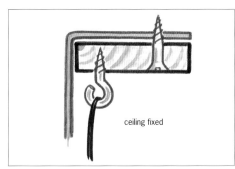

ceiling fixed

3

5

Step 3

With the pleating lines now marked on the blind, mark the positions for the rings to be sewn for the cording system. Rings should be sewn on each line 5 cm (2 in) from each outer edge and at intervals of 20–30 cm (8–12 in). Hand sew the rings firmly through both layers of the fabric using a thread that matches the colouring of the top fabric. Rub out the chalk lines.

Day Two
Step 4

Prepare the wooden batten, covering it with lining fabric and screwing the screw eyelets into it to line up with the rings sewn to the blind. Add an extra screw eyelet to the side that the cords are to pull from.

Step 5

Lay the blind face down and attach the batten to the top of the blind using staples or tacks (on the top of the board if the blind is to hang from the ceiling, or on the back edge of the board if it is to be attached to the wall). Check that the drop is correct and that the blind hangs straight before cording the blind and fixing the batten to the window, wall or ceiling.

Step 6

Tie a length of nylon cord to each of the rings at the base of the blind and run the cord up through the rings above and along the screw eyelets attached to the batten. Extend the cord approximately halfway down the blind either to the left or to the right, depending upon which side the blind is to be pulled up from. At a convenient height and to the side of the wall that the cords are to fall, screw on the cleat. Pull up the blind and arrange the folds. Then level off the cords, thread them through the acorn, and knot them together before cleating the cords to hold up the blind.

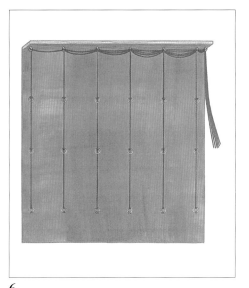

6

Roman blind

Roman blinds, with their clean and sophisticated lines, are folded into even horizontal pleats when drawn up. Wooden poles fitted at intervals along the back keep these pleats straight.

Roman blinds will suit a variety of different windows and room settings. When hung alone at a window they give a feeling of space and simplicity. When hung with dress (mock) curtains, though, a more elegant look can be achieved. They may also be used in a run of two or three if the window itself is very large.

As Roman blinds take up so little space when they are pulled up, they are a most suitable choice for windows with only a limited amount of surrounding wall space, whether this is above the window frame (as in many bays) or at the sides.

These blinds may be set inside a window recess, or on the wall or ceiling outside it. They are simple to fit, simple to make, and use very little fabric.

A successful Roman blind can be made from most fabrics - thick or thin, plain or patterned. Take account of the size and shape of the window when choosing a patterned fabric, however; one or two complete vases of flowers, for instance, will look much better than one and part of another. Always position any stripes evenly across the blind.

Planning your time

DAY ONE
AM: Cut out top fabric and lining, machine sew them together

PM: Cut out pockets for the poles and sew to the blind; check required lengths of wooden dowelling; hand sew plastic rings to back of blind

DAY TWO
AM: Prepare and position top hanging board, cut wooden poles to fit pockets

PM: String blind and hang, fix cleat to wall

Tools and materials

Top fabric

Lining fabric

Matching sewing threads

Lengths of 12 mm (½ in) diameter wooden dowelling (approximately 4–8 lengths)

20–40 small plastic rings

Nylon cord (approximately 10–12 times the length of the blind)

5 x 2 cm (2 x ¾ in) wooden batten cut to the same measurement as the width of the blind

Angle brackets and screws to fix batten

Screw eyelets (between 4 and 6)

Brass cleat

Acorn or similar to keep the cord ends together

Basic sewing kit

Large pair of scissors

Sewing machine

Metre ruler and metal tape measure

Soft pencil

Tacks and hammer or staples and staple gun

Drill, screwdriver, screws and wallplugs

Small saw

Preparation

Decide on the position of the blind – is it to hang inside the window recess, or outside it on the wall or ceiling? Measure up for top fabric and lining (see below).

Measuring up for fabrics

Inside the recess: Measure across the window (from wall to wall) for the width and add 3 cm (1¼ in) for seams. Measure from the top of the window to the sill (the 'drop') and add 10–15 cm (4–6 in) for seams and hanging allowance.

Outside the recess: Measure across the window, allowing at least 5 cm (2 in) of overlap onto the wall on each side, plus 3 cm (1¼ in) for seams. Decide on the height of the blind, which should be no more than 15 cm (6 in) above the recess. Measure from this point to the sill if it protrudes, or a minimum of 5 cm (2 in) below if it does not. Add 10–15 cm (4–6 in) to this drop measurement for the seams and hanging allowance.

As most furnishing fabrics are 137 cm (54 in) wide (see Terms and techniques – Furnishing fabrics) one width of fabric will be adequate for almost all Roman blinds. You will therefore need to buy a length of top fabric to the measurement of the drop plus seam and hanging allowances. If a large patterned fabric is being used, buy

extra fabric to allow the pattern to be positioned on the blind as you want it. Roman blinds should be lined using a tightly woven cotton sateen lining fabric or alternatively a plain-coloured glazed chintz (see Terms and techniques – Linings). For your blind you will need the same amount of lining fabric as top fabric plus 150 cm (59 in) for the pole pockets.

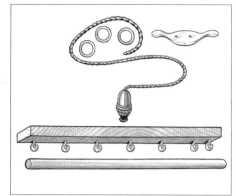

Day One
Step 1

Cut out the top fabric to the measurements of the window plus the allowances, taking care to cut the fabric accurately along the grain (see Terms and techniques – Grain), centralizing and positioning any pattern. Cut out the lining fabric to exactly the same measurements as the top fabric.

Lay the top fabric flat on a table, face up. Lay the lining, face down, on the top. Smooth out all wrinkles and creases from the two fabrics and pin them together, leaving a 1.5 cm (⅝ in) seam allowance. Then machine sew down both sides and along the base.

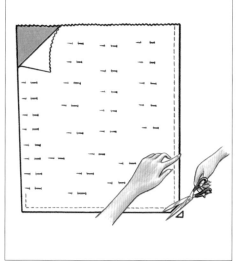

1

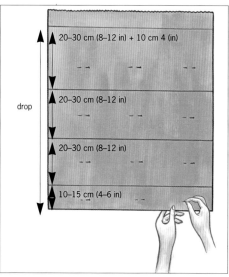

2

Step 2

Remove all pins, trim the corners and turn the blind the right way out. Press the blind, taking care to press out and flatten the seams.

Lay the blind flat, this time with the lining face up, and pin the two layers together all over. Draw a pencil line across the blind, marking off the drop measurement. It is below this line that you should mark the sewing lines for the pockets to hold the wooden poles.

Each pleat or fold needs a wooden pole to support the fabric from behind, and pockets need to be made from the lining fabric to cover them. Rings are then sewn to these pockets to carry the cording system.

For pleats of 10-15 cm (4-6 in) deep, the poles should hang 20-30 cm (8-12 in) apart. There should be an allowance of approximately 10 cm (4 in) at the top of the blind (incorporated in the top pleat) to accommodate the

screw eyelets and the cording system. The rest of the blind should be divided equally by 20-30 cm (8-12 in), allowing for a 'pleat' of 10-15 cm (4-6 in) at the base. Draw pencil lines across the blind at these points.

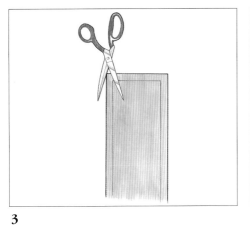

3

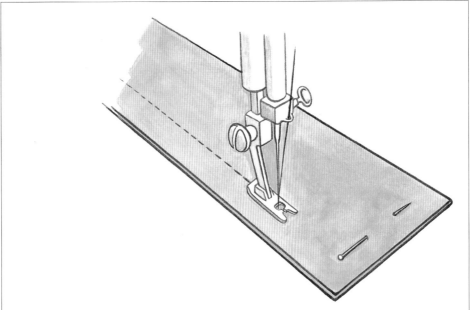

4

Step 3

To make up the pockets to hold the poles, cut strips of lining fabric 10 cm (4 in) wide and as long as the blind is wide. If possible cut these strips from the length of the fabric rather than across the width as the weave is tighter and the pockets will wear better. Cut as many strips as you have marked sewing lines on your blind.

Step 4

Fold in and press a seam allowance of approx 12 mm (½ in) all around each strip of fabric. Fold the strip in half widthways and pin the open edges together. Machine sew one side and along the length.

Step 5

Pin the folded side of the pockets to the pencil lines, setting the pockets approx 12 mm (½ in) from each side of the blind. Thread up the sewing machine with threads to match both the top fabric and lining, and check the tension (see Terms and techniques – Checking tension). Sew the pockets to the blind along the pencil markings. The machine stitching should be as unobtrusive as possible on the front of the blind.

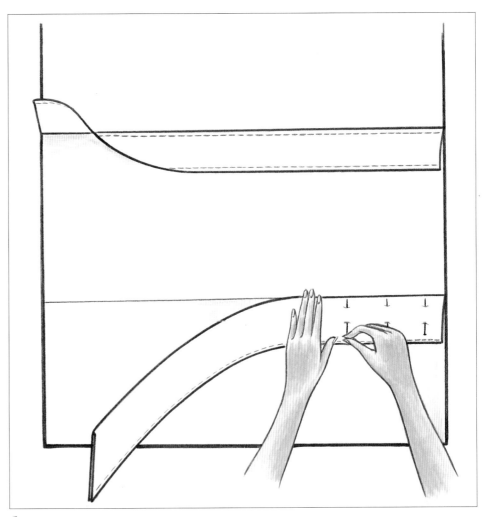

5

Step 6

Cut the wooden dowelling into lengths 3 cm (1¼ in) less than the width of the blind. Slide them into the pockets and hand sew the open ends. Hand sew the plastic rings to the outer edges of the pockets. These should be positioned in rows down the blind, 5 cm (2 in) from each side and at 20-40 cm (8-15¾ in) intervals across the blind.

Day Two
Step 7

Prepare the wooden batten, covering it with lining fabric and screwing in the screw eyelets to line up with the plastic rings sewn to the blind. Add an extra screw eyelet to the side that the cords are to pull from. Lay the blind face down and attach the batten to the top of the blind using staples or tacks. Check that the drop is correct and that the blind hangs straight before cording the blind and fixing the batten to the window, wall or ceiling using one of the two methods shown, (a) or (b).

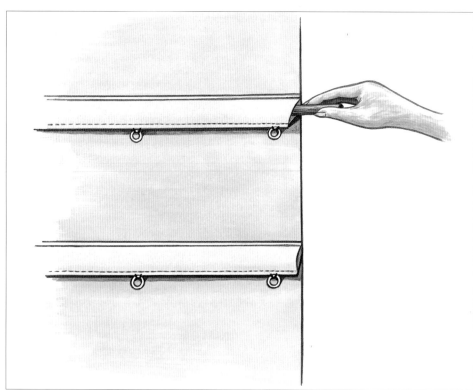

6

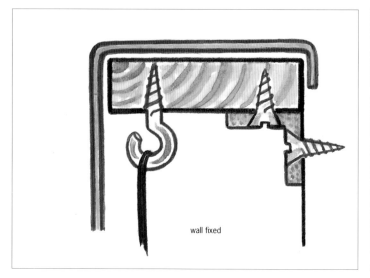

wall fixed

7a

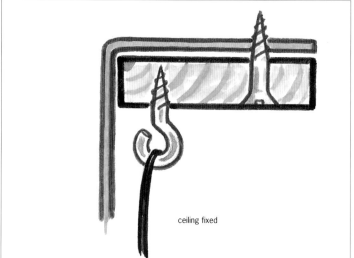

ceiling fixed

7b

Step 8

To cord the blind tie a length of nylon cord to each of the rings at the base of the blind; run the cords through the rings above and along the screw eyelets on the batten. Extend the cord to approximately halfway down the blind either to the left or to the right, depending on which side the blind is to pull up from.

Step 9

At a convenient height and to the side of the wall that the cords are to fall, screw on the cleat. Pull up the blind, arrange the folds, and level off the cords. Then thread the cords through the acorn, knot them together and cleat the cords.

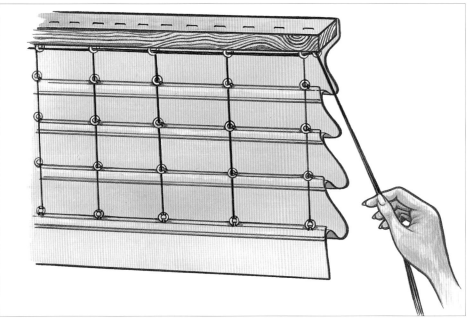

8

Fitting blinds together

Where you are fitting a row of Roman blinds together, as on a large window or in a bay, the blinds should butt together at the sides.

Make sure that all the pleating is identical, with the poles running in a continuous line, and that the pattern on the fabric is at the same level. This also applies to blinds hung on different windows but in the same room.

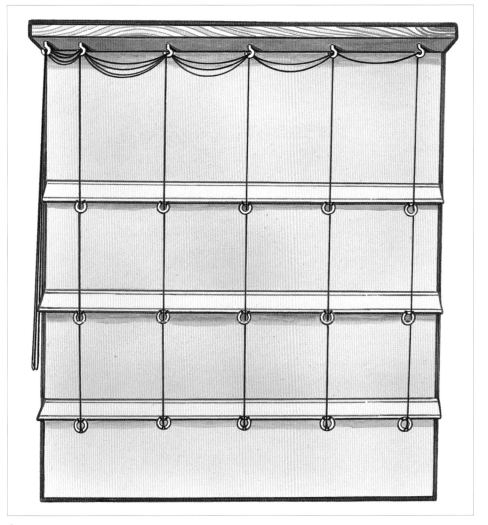

9

Pelmet

A deep pelmet fitted above a window makes a stylish heading and can add height to a room. Here I have teamed up a decorative pelmet with a blind in complementary colours.

Pelmets and lambrequins act as headings or frames for a window and can be used either with curtains or blinds, or on their own. The depth at the centre of both pelmets and lambrequins should measure at least one sixth of either the curtain drop or the window height. They may be made straight, with an even depth, or be shaped. While pelmets and lambrequins are made in similar ways, lambrequins are generally larger and require a firmer base. Pelmets may be made with a buckram base (a form of stiffened hessian) while lambrequins require a base of wood. Fabrics may be stapled to these wooden bases but must be sewn or glued onto softer bases.

Pelmets and lambrequins can be fitted directly onto a wall (across the window recess) or can be hung from a pelmet board that extends out over the curtains or blinds. They should be fixed with Velcro or angle brackets, depending on the weight that they are to support.

When designing the shape of a pelmet or lambrequin, follow the pattern of the fabric, or be inspired by other features of the room; for example, the lines of the furniture or the patterns of a rug or other furnishings.

Planning your time

DAY ONE

AM: Make up pelmet board or fix Velcro or angle brackets to wall, cut pelmet buckram or wood to shape

PM: Cut out fabric and wadding, cover front of board with wadding and fabric

DAY TWO

AM: Cover back with lining fabric, sew Velcro to back or screw on angle brackets; fix pelmet to wall or board

Tools and materials

Top fabric (see Measuring up, page 68)

Wadding: 55 or 110 g (2 or 4 oz) (measurements as top fabric)

Lining fabric (measurements as top fabric)

Matching sewing threads

Pelmet buckram (heavy duty and impregnated with an adhesive if available)

Fabric adhesive (PVA-based or Copydex)

2 cm (¾ in) thick board (see Measuring up pelmet board, page 68)

2 or more angle brackets and screws (depending on the span of the board)

2 interlocking strips of Velcro to cover the length of the pelmet

Basic sewing kit

Heavy duty craft scissors or craft knife

Sewing machine

Metre ruler and metal tape measure

Soft pencil

Pegs

Curved needle

Iron and ironing board

Drill, screwdriver, screws and wallplugs

Preparation

Decide whether the pelmet is to be fixed directly onto the wall or onto a pelmet board. Measure up for pelmet board and fabric (see below).

Design the pelmet and make a paper template. Temporarily fix the paper template in position over the window and check that the desired effect is achieved. Decide how padded the pelmet should be.

Measuring up for pelmet board

If you are fitting your pelmet away from the window recess and fixing it to a board, the board will need to be approximately 10 cm (4 in) wide (wider if it is to cover heavy curtains, due to the stack back, but narrower if the pelmet is to cover a simple roller blind). The length should be approximately 5 cm (2 in) longer than any curtain track (2.5 cm [1 in] at each end).

Measuring up for buckram

Width: Pelmet buckram is available in various widths. Measure the depth of the pelmet and buy buckram of a width to accommodate this depth measurement at its deepest point.

Length: For a pelmet that is to lie flat against the wall, add

approximately 15 cm (6 in) to the width of the window recess to obtain the correct length. For a pelmet that is to be fixed to a board, measure the length of the board plus the returns (see Terms and techniques – Return) at each end (see also *Preventing a pelmet board from bowing* on page 69).

Measuring up for fabric

The amount of fabric required depends on how the pattern of the fabric is to be used – use your paper template to plan this out. If it is necessary to join widths, do not forget to allow for the pattern repeat (see Terms and techniques – Pattern repeats). Finally, allow an extra 3 cm (1¼ in) all around to cover the edges (that is, add 6 cm [2½ in] to the overall length and 6 cm [2½ in] to the width).

Day One
Step 1

Cut the pelmet board to size, and paint it or cover with lining fabric. Fix it to the wall with the angle brackets and glue or staple one of the Velcro strips to the outside edge of the board OR Glue the strip of Velcro to the wall above the window recess, extending it to each side.

1a Covered board fixed to wall with angle brackets.

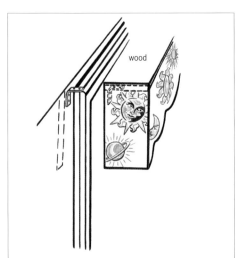

1b Finished pelmet with 'returns'.

1c Velcro stuck to wall to receive Velcro on pelmet.

Step 2

Check the paper template for accuracy of shape and outline.

Step 3

Lay the buckram flat and draw round the shape of the pelmet from the paper template.

Step 4

Cut out the buckram, not forgetting to add on any returns.

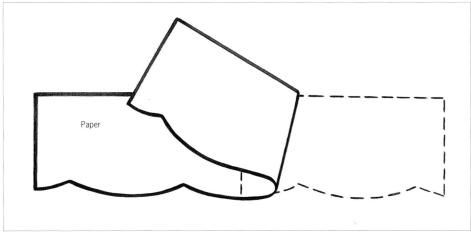

2

Preventing a pelmet board from bowing

A large and deep pelmet fixed to a board can be prevented from bowing by extending the buckram by 5 cm (2 in) at each end and giving the returns themselves returns. Tuck these behind the board against the wall and tack them down. Here, Velcro would be too bulky.

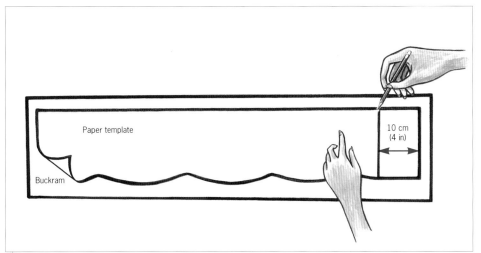

3

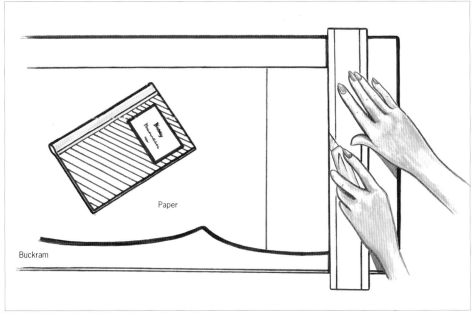

4

Step 5

Lay the buckram flat (it may be necessary to put weights at either end to stop it curling up) and cover with wadding (either 55 or 110 g – 2 or 4 oz), depending on the 'look' you require). The wadding should have an allowance of 3 cm (1¼ in) all around to cover the edges. It should be stretched over the buckram and glued in position (or ironed on if the buckram is impregnated with an adhesive).

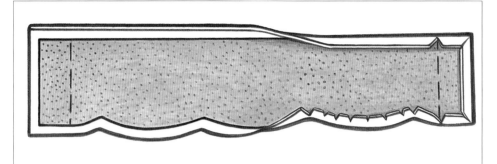

5

Step 6

Making sure that the grain (see Terms and techniques – Grain) of the fabric is lying straight along the pelmet and that the pattern is correctly positioned, cover the wadded buckram with the top fabric. The fabric should be fairly tight and free of wrinkles, but not so tight that the wadding is flattened. Using pegs to keep the top fabric in place, glue the excess fabric to the back of the pelmet, cutting the fabric according to the shape of the buckram.

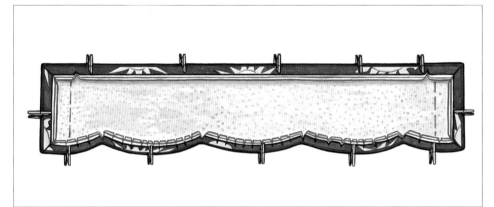

6

Piping

Piping is a good edging for a pelmet, and it is relatively easy to make by covering piping cord with a length of fabric that has been cut on the bias – that is across the fabric grain. Cutting it this way makes the strip more pliable and less likely to pucker round the shaped edges of a pelmet. To cut strips of bias fabric, fold down the selvedge of a width of fabric (approximately 40 cm [15¾ in] in length) to lie parallel with the cut edge and press down. This diagonal fold line is the first cutting line. Draw lines parallel to this at distances of approximately 8–10 cm (3⅛–4 in) apart. Cut the strips and join them together by placing the right sides of the fabric together with the strips forming a V shape. Wrap the bias strip around the cord and align the raw edges, pinning at regular intervals. Using the zipper foot on the machine, stitch down alongside the cord. Do not sew too near the cord, as the stitching should not show when the piping is in place. Glue the seam allowance on the piping to the back of the pelmet, with the cord-filled fabric only showing from the front, following the contours of the pelmet. Where the angles are particularly sharp, snip into the seam allowance to ease the piping around them. Stitch the lining to the back of the pelmet right up to the piping cord, hiding the stitches between the layers of the cord and the bias strip.

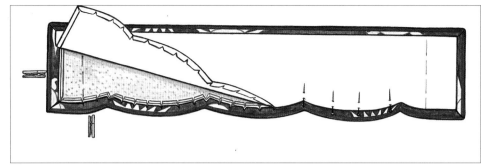

7

Day Two
Step 7

Cut out the lining fabric, joining strips together if necessary. When the glue on the back of the pelmet is dry, remove the pegs and pin the lining in place; starting from the middle and working towards the ends, turn the rough edges under and pin the lining approximately 1 cm (½ in) from the edge all around.

Step 8

Hand sew the lining to the top fabric using a small curved needle. Either glue or hand sew the other strip of Velcro to the top edge of the back of the pelmet. Fix the pelmet to the wall or the pelmet board using the two opposing Velcro strips.

To keep a particularly deep pelmet flush with the wall, fix Velcro to the sides of the pelmet and wall as well as to the top edge. Press the blind firmly in place.

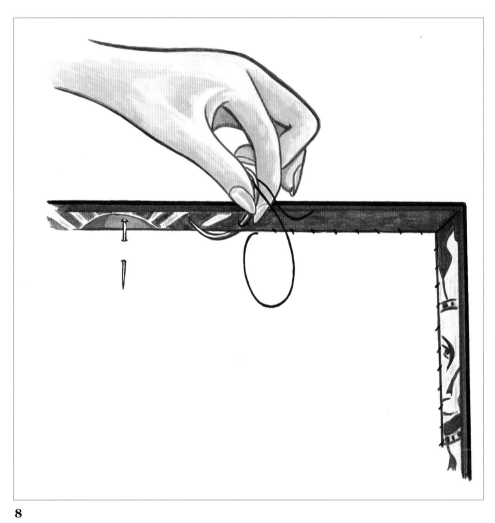

8

Quilted fabrics

Quilted fabrics can look very good as a covering for pelmets or lambrequins. Choose a fabric with a definite pattern, such as a check or stripe or a small flower. To quilt the fabric, first back the fabric with wadding and a lining and pin the layers together. Then tack the layers together keeping the top fabric as smooth as possible. The lines of tacking should radiate from the centre of the piece of fabric. Now machine stitch around or along the pattern using a very large stitch, again starting from the middle and working towards the outer edges. Cut the original piece of fabric slightly larger than you need as there will be some 'take up' (see Terms and techniques) of the material.

Lambrequin

A lambrequin fitted on its own, with its extended sides, can give an otherwise ordinary window some interest and decoration. I chose a rich-looking fabric for an Eastern theme.

L ambrequin - a short piece of drapery over a door or window, pronounced 'lamperkin'. This was the original definition. Nowadays it means a shaped board covered in a flat piece of fabric, to be fitted over a door or window.

Fashion has indeed repeated itself. The first lambrequins became popular in the 19th century after the excesses of the previous age with its abundant use of drapings and frills. They are now popular again following on from the fashion for swags and tails. Now interior design generally has become much more streamlined.

Design the lambrequin so that its sides cover the complete drop if the window is small, or a minimum of one third of the drop if the window is large. Shape the centre to take account of the theme of the room or the printed pattern on the top fabric and make up a paper template.

When a lambrequin is to be used in conjunction with curtains or blinds and is to sit outside the recess, it needs to be fixed to a pelmet board. Otherwise it can be made to fit over the window recess and flush to the wall or to fit inside the recess itself.

Planning your time

DAY ONE
AM: Make up pelmet board and fix to wall; cut chipboard to shape

PM: Cut out fabric and wadding; cover front of board with wadding and fabric

DAY TWO
AM: Staple lining fabric to back of board

PM: Fix the angle brackets to the back of the lambrequin and fix to the wall or onto the board

Tools and materials

Top fabric (see Measuring up, page 74)

Wadding: 55 or 110 g (2 or 4 oz) (measurements as top fabric)

Lining fabric (measurements as top fabric)

Matching sewing threads

12 mm (½ in) chipboard

Fabric adhesive (PVA-based or Copydex)

2 cm (¾ in) board – for the pelmet board, fitting outside a recess only

2 or 4 angle brackets and screws

Basic sewing kit

Sewing machine (only if fabric widths are to be joined)

Metre ruler and metal tape measure

Staple gun and staples

Curved needle

Drill, screwdriver, screws and wallplugs

Preparation

Design lambrequin and make up a paper template.

Measuring up for pelmet board

See Pelmet, page 68.

Measuring for a wooden frame

With its extended sides, the lambrequin needs a stronger base than the pelmet. The best choice is chipboard. Plywood and MDF are suitable but very heavy. Hardboard, though light, does not take staples very well.

If the lambrequin is to sit outside the window recess it will fix to a pelmet board and will need side panels. Cut these slightly narrower than the returns on the pelmet board to allow for the thickness of the wadding and top fabric. These side panels should then be fixed to the front panel and checked for size before it is covered with fabric.

Measuring up for fabric

See Pelmet, page 68.

Cut the fabric with an allowance of 5 cm (2 in) all around for the edges (rather than the 3 cm (1¼ in) allowance used for pelmets). Chipboard is thicker than buckram.

Day One
Step 1

If the lambrequin is to fit outside the window recess, cut a pelmet board to size and either paint it or cover it with lining fabric. Fix it to the wall with the angle brackets.

Check the paper template for accuracy of shape and outline (see Pelmet, Step 2, page 69).

Cut the chipboard to shape and, where necessary, make allowances for the fabric thicknesses. Fit side panels only if the lambrequin is to be fixed outside the recess. Cover the chipboard with wadding – a thin layer of adhesive will help to keep the wadding in place. Cut out the top fabric using the paper template as a pattern, and adding a 5 cm (2 in) allowance all around. Check that the pattern on the fabric is positioned correctly and that the grain is straight (see Terms and techniques – Grain). Stretch the fabric firmly over the wadding and staple to the back of the chipboard. There should be an even allowance of top fabric showing around the back edge.

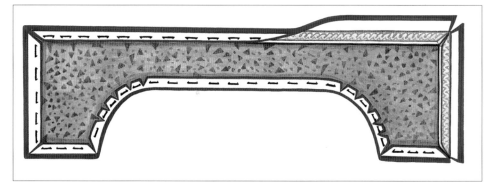

1

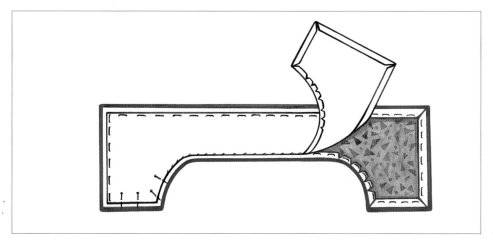

2

Step 2

Cut out the lining fabric and, starting from the centre of each edge, pin the lining in place, turning the rough edges under as you go. Continue pinning until the lining is smooth, straight and fits tightly all around.

Day Two

Step 3

Staple the lining in place, placing the staples as near to the edge of the lining fabric as possible.

Step 4

If the lambrequin is to be in such a position that the staples on the bottom edge can be seen from the front, hand sew this part using a curved needle.

Step 5

Fix sufficient angle brackets to the back of the lambrequin to hold the weight and then attach them to the pelmet board (see Pelmet, Step 1, page 68) or to the inside of the window recess.

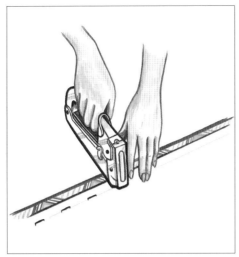

3

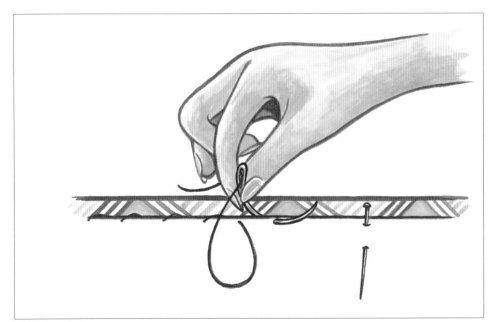

4

Adding fringing

If you are fixing fringing to the edge or edges of the pelmet or lambrequin, make allowances for the fabric pattern, as the braid may cover more of the pattern than you want it to. Fringing or braids can be hand sewn or glued in place.

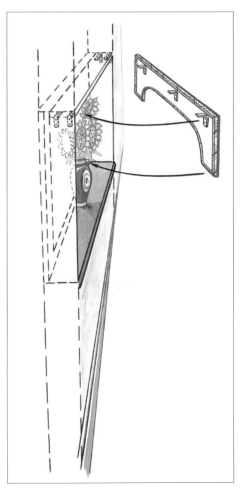

5

Terms and techniques

Back stitch

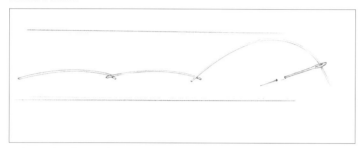

A large back stitch or prick stitch is used on the side seams of curtains. This stitch fastens together the layers of fabric with only minimal thread showing on the front of the fabric. It is quick and easy to sew.

Working from left to right and with the needle pointing to the left, pick up just two or three threads of the fabric, then bring the thread back 2–3 cm (¾–1¼ in) and pick up two or three more threads and so on. Do not pull the thread too tightly or the fabric may pucker.

Basic sewing kit

This should consist of:
A pair of large, sharp scissors for fabrics.
A pair of large, old scissors for craftwork.
A pair of small needlework scissors.
An unpicker.
Several packets of glass or plastic-headed pins.
A selection of long sewing needles.

Other useful, though not essential, tools are a hand-held staple gun and a hot-melt glue gun.

Buckram

Used as a stiffener for pelmets and tiebacks, buckram is made from a hessian that has been stiffened with size. It is available in several weights and is sometimes available impregnated with a glue, so that fabric sticks to it when it is ironed. Heading buckram, used mainly for handsewn curtain headings, is softer, 13 cm (5 in) wide and made from cotton stiffened with size.

Checking tension

Before starting machine stitching on any of these projects, check the tension of the threads. Test the machine with two different coloured threads, one colour on the top, and with the bobbin threaded up with the second colour. Make sure that only one colour shows from the front of the fabric, with the second colour only showing on the back. Alter the tension accordingly. It is always worth starting each project with a new sewing machine needle.

Cut length

The length of fabric cut before it is made into a curtain; that is, the finished length of the curtain, plus the allowances for hems and turnings.

'Dress' the curtain

Achieving the perfect 'stack back' for curtains.
When the curtains are first hung, push them back tightly. Arrange the folds vertically from heading to hem, one fold for each hook, and tie soft tapes around them in three places down the curtain. Leave them for a day or two tied with the tapes before releasing and pulling. From now on each time the curtains draw back they should fall automatically into the original folds.

Drop

The finished length of the curtain.

Flat fell seams

To join two widths of fabric together and for the raw edge to be hidden as is required for an unlined curtain, a flat fell seam should be used. Join the lengths and match the pattern, matching the pattern at least 4 cm (1½ in) in from the selvedges. Cut off one length of selvedge by trimming the 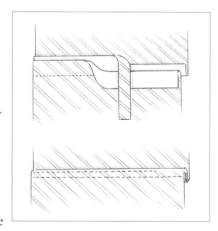 seam to 1 cm (½ in), trim the other seam to 2.5 cm (1 in) and fold it over and under the first seam. Press it well and machine stitch down the full length as near to the edge of the fold as possible.

Furnishing fabrics

Furnishing fabrics have always been woven in two widths, 122 cm (48 in) and 137 cm (54 in). Nowadays, though, there are far fewer available in 122 cm (48 in) widths, and many more that measure 140 cm (55 in) wide.

While the choice of fabric is a personal matter with regard to colour and pattern, be careful to choose a fabric that is tightly woven and is fairly thick. Do not choose any fabric that is stiff with dressing; this will soon evaporate, leaving the fabric limp and liable to creasing. Check that the fabric is soft enough to fall into folds easily and drapes well. A thick, soft cotton fabric is the simplest to work with and will always give the best results.

Grain

The lengthwise (warp) and the crosswise (weft) threads of fabric should be woven at right angles on the fabric. These are the grain lines, and the patterns on the fabric should be printed to follow these lines exactly.

Hemming stitch

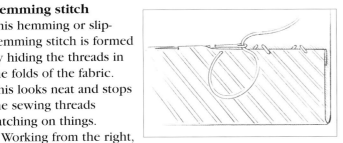

This hemming or slip-hemming stitch is formed by hiding the threads in the folds of the fabric. This looks neat and stops the sewing threads catching on things.

Working from the right, fasten the sewing thread, catch two or three threads of the flat fabric and then insert the needle inside the folded edge, sliding it along for about 1-2 cm (½-¾ in). Bring the needle out of the fold and catch two or three threads from the flat fabric immediately opposite the emerging needle. Continue along the hem in this way. Every now and again check that the stitches are almost invisible on the front surface. Do not pull the thread too tightly.

Interlinings

There are several interlinings available. The thickest one, known as 'Bump', is made from cotton waste; difficult to handle, it is also difficult to care for. Domette is also made of cotton, but is very thin. By far the easiest to use and the most adaptable is a synthetic interlining made from nylon and Sarill cotton mixture. This clings to top fabric and therefore lies very smooth. Synthetic interlining can also be cleaned and washes well if necessary.

Joining widths

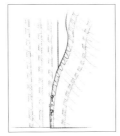

To join two widths of fabric and for the patterns to match, lay the two lengths face up with the selvedges together, fold and press one side in to include approximately 2 cm (¾ in) of pattern, or 4-5 cm (1½-2 in) if a flat fell seam is

subsequently to be formed. Place this onto the other length of fabric, matching up the pattern as the two pieces are pinned together.

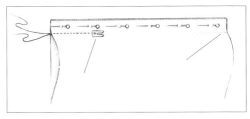

Fold the top length over so that the two lengths are lying with right sides together, and pin the selvedges together. Remove the pins from the front of the curtain and, turning the fabric back over, machine sew down the length of the crease line showing on the back of the fabric. Check that the patterns are perfectly matched before cutting off the selvedges and pressing the seam open.

Ladder stitch

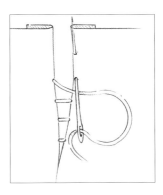

This stitch is used to join two folded edges together. Secure the thread inside one folded edge and then cross over the opening into the opposite fold. Make a stitch 0.5 cm (¼ in) long and pull the needle through into the other fold again. Work backwards and forwards across the gap inserting the needle just inside the fold of the fabric. Pull the thread and close the gap before fastening off. The stitches should be invisible.

Linings

Curtain linings are produced in the same widths as furnishing fabrics and the same principles as to quality apply to lining fabrics. They should be fairly thick and not stiff with dressing. Choose a shade such as white, ivory or beige to match any background on the top fabric, or a shade to match the rest of the curtain linings in the house. Coloured lining fabrics tend to fade quickly; a glazed chintz fabric used dull side up will last longer.

Lock stitch

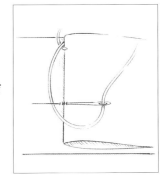

This stitch is used to keep two layers of fabric connected. The stitches should be very loose and widely spaced. The fabrics should be able to move independently of each other.

Choose a thread to match the colour of the top fabric and, with the lining fabric folded over in half lengthways, catch a few threads of the fold of the lining and two or three threads of the top fabric. Make a loop of thread before making the next stitch 20 cm (8 in) down the fold, taking the needle over the thread.

Rows of these stitches should be worked down the lengths of lined and interlined curtains at every half width of fabric.

Pattern repeats

Patterns printed on fabrics are repeated evenly throughout the roll. These repeat measurements will be on the manufacturer's label, but can easily be measured. Repeated patterns are usually either

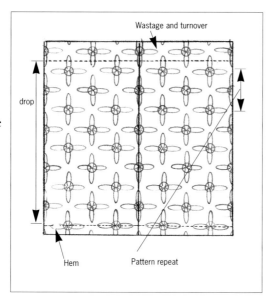

16¼ cm (6¼ in), 32 cm (12¾ in), or 64 cm (26 in) apart. When joining two widths of a patterned fabric, the pattern must be matched up. This is achieved by dividing the sum of the drop and hem and top allowance (drop plus 20 cm [8 in]) measurement by the pattern repeat measurement, and rounding it up to a whole number of repeats. Each cut length must be made up of completed patterns. Each width cut will now be identical in pattern, so that the widths will match when they are joined together to make the curtains.

Return

The part of the curtain heading that turns around the end of the track towards the wall.

Selvedge

The sides of the curtain fabric that are strengthened by using extra and tighter threads. These selvedges should be cut off once the fabric lengths have been cut out and joined together. On curtain linings they may be just snipped to release any tension.

Take-up

When layers of fabric are sewn together, the through sewing will cause indentations and so make the overall size of the fabric pieces smaller.

Tapes

'Standard tape' is 4 cm (1½ in) wide and will gather up the fabric in an unstructured fashion.

'Pencil pleat tape' is 8 cm (3⅛ in) wide and will gather up the curtain fabric in a much more precise way, forming neat rows of pencil-size channels.

It is always better to buy a cotton tape rather than one made in a synthetic material as synthetic tape will slip around and stretch as it is being sewn. It is also worth choosing a tape that has fabric pockets for the hooks rather than rows of strings. The strings 'give' and gradually the curtains drop nearer the ground or sill with more of the hanging showing at the top.

Tracks and poles

There are numerous different types and styles of tracks and poles available, and it will be personal choice that is the deciding factor. Choose a pole with a wide diameter or a metal track rather than a plastic track for heavy curtains. If the track is to show it can be painted to match the wall. Always hang the track or pole well above the window and extend it beyond the window at each side.

Waddings

Terylene waddings, made in different weights (and therefore thicknesses) are widely available and are suitable as interlining for a small project such as swags, but not for large curtains.

Work space

All these projects will be completed far more easily and enjoyably in the right working conditions. Choose an uncluttered area that has good light, preferably daylight, a comfortable seat and a large table so that you can keep your tools and materials to hand.

The table does not need to be particularly large: a kitchen or dining table is nearly always adequate. It does, though, need to be set at the correct height for working. Build up the table by placing bricks or books under each leg to make it worktop height. Protect any polished surfaces with a heavy cloth. If possible have the sewing machine on a small table to the side. A steam iron and ironing board will also be needed for pressing seams and finishing projects.

Suppliers

Thanks to the following for providing products for this book:

ARC Prints
103 Wandsworth Bridge Road
London SW6 2TE
Tel. 0171 731 3933
Pictures - pages 29 and 47

Damask
3-4 Broxholme House
New King's Road
London SW6 4AA
Tel. 0171 731 3553
Hanger and nightdress -
page 25

Deptich Designs
7 College Fields
Prince George's Road
London SW19 2PT
Tel. 0181 687 0867
Dressing table and stool -
page 25

McCloud & Co
269 Wandsworth Bridge Road
London SW6 2TX
Tel. 0171 371 7151
Console table and candlesticks -
page 47

Meaker & Son
166 Wandsworth Bridge Road
London SW6
Tel. 0171 731 7416
Cane and pine furniture -
pages 9, 29 and 37

The Pier
91-95 Kings Road
London SW3 4PA
Tel. 0171 351 7100
Chair - page 73

Pukka Palace
174 Tower Bridge Road
London SE1 3LS
Tel. 0171 234 0000
Furniture and accessories - pages 67
and 73

Sanderson
Tel. 0171 584 3344 for stockists
Paint

Index